THE OLD TESTAMENT:

A MORMON PERSPECTIVE

THE OLD TESTAMENT:

A MORMON PERSPECTIVE

GLENN L. PEARSON

Bookcraft
Salt Lake City, Utah

Library of Congress Catalog Card Number: 80:68069
ISBN 0-88494-406-9

First Printing, 1980

Lithographed in the United States of America
PUBLISHERS PRESS
Salt Lake City, Utah

To Ardith

CONTENTS

ACKNOWLEDGMENTS

I owe a special debt of gratitude to the many colleagues who have touched and strengthened my life through thirty-two years of experience in the Church Education System.

I express appreciation to Richard Draper, on whom I leaned for large segments of the first drafts; and to Lois Beshears for having typed much of the manuscript, frequently under time pressures.

I am particularly grateful to my wife for her total patience while the book was being written.

1

The First and the Last

The Old Testament just might be the last book as well as the first. It is first in terms of time, since it covers the first thirty-six hundred years of human history as well as giving some vague and general comments on the Creation. (That is, they are vague in most ways, though very specific in other ways.) It is last because, for most Christians, it is the hardest to read. And, for most Latter-day Saints, it is the last and the least read of all the standard works. But it may be last in another sense—in the sense that it is the last great treasure-house of the mysteries of God that Latter-day Saint scholars (scholars in the best priesthood sense, not in the secular sense) turn to when they have comprehended quite well the rest of the standard works. Then it becomes a priesthood handbook, a companion to the

Doctrine and Covenants. So, in this sense, being last means being first.

To appreciate this handbook idea one needs to have some understanding of the history of the Jews. The Old Testament has been a handbook to them for thousands of years. Even the most liberal of Jews are governed in their daily lives by the Old Testament to an extent far beyond anything a non-Jew can imagine. They—the Jews in general, that is—study it not only to learn what rules are spelled out in the form of commandments or instructions, but also to learn how the ancients interpreted or practiced those instructions and commandments. Through the generations that have passed since Ezra in the sixth century B.C., the Jews have accumulated a vast commentary on the Old Testament.

Even non-Jews have been influenced by this vast commentary far more than they may realize. For instance, the English Common Law is essentially biblical law as worked out by generations of Jews. And the United States Constitution is essentially an Old Testament document.

One reason why the Old Testament is hard to understand is that its earliest writings were handed down for many centuries until, at last, they were edited and compiled into a book sometime between 550 B.C. and 450 B.C. Many precious things had been lost or destroyed. But as far as plainness and completeness are concerned, the book of that day—the so-called postexilic day—was a much better book than the one we have now. We know this from what we learn in 1 Nephi 6 about the brass plates of Laban and from what we learn in 1 Nephi 13 about the Bible of Jesus' day. It was a truly Jewish book, however, speaking in a national and cultural sense. And it continued that way until after the time of Jesus. Thus Nephi could say of that book which Jesus' apostles promulgated, "[the book] proceedeth out of the mouth of a Jew" (1 Nephi 13:24). Since the days of the apostles, besides the loss of the plain and precious things (1 Nephi 13:26-29), the Bible has come to us out of the mouths of Greeks, Englishmen and others.

The New Testament aside—that is, leaving its textual problems out of this discussion—our Old Testament is a translation from Hebrew texts that are fairly recent—only about a thousand years old—and from the Greek Septuagint, which is much more ancient in terms of continuously existing manuscripts, even though it originally was a translation of older Hebrew manuscripts which are no longer in existence. Both the Hebrew and the Greek texts have become somewhat corrupted, though they flowed through different channels from the same originally pure fountain of long ago. The miracle is that both the Hebrew and the Greek versions still are such great witnesses of each other and of the Lord's providence in preserving what he wanted us to have.

The official attitude of The Church of Jesus Christ of Latter-day Saints is that the Bible is the word of God "as far as it is translated correctly." This does not mean that we believe the Bible less than other churches believe it. Neither the Jews nor the Christians believe the Bible as literally or completely as do the Latter-day Saints. Besides this, those who criticize our position are hopelessly inconsistent, because they all have been involved in translation and research to increase knowledge of what the original texts may have said. Dr. Adam Clarke, whose famous commentary on the Old and New Testaments was in its final form before 1830, was fundamental in his approach to the Bible. That is, he believed it to be the absolute word of God, a divine revelation. Yet he didn't hesitate to discuss the problems of translation and transmission of biblical texts. With reference to the manuscripts of the book of Ezekiel, Clarke wrote:

> The ancient *Versions* give some help; but it is astonishing how difficult it is to settle the text by a collation of MSS. This has not yet been properly done; and we cannot know the *true meaning* till we can ascertain the *true reading*. But after having laboured in this way, I must express myself as the learned professor of the oriental tongues at Parma, J. B. De Rossi: . . . "That there is so much inconstancy and variation among the MSS., especially in the *suffixed pronouns,* that I was weary of my labour; and I could more truly say of the whole book of Ezekiel, than Norzius did relative to one passage in Zechariah, who, bitterly complaining of the many variations he met with, said, 'My soul was perplexed with them, and I turned away my face from them.' " As most of our printed editions have been taken from a very inadequate collation of MSS., especially of this prophet, much remains to be done to restore the text to a proper state of purity. When this is done it is presumed that several of the difficulties in this book will be removed. In many instances Abp. Newcome has been very successful. (Adam Clarke, *The Holy Bible Containing the Old and New Testaments*, 6 vols. [Nashville: Abingdon Press, n.d.], 4:419; hereafter cited as Clarke.)

Clarke apparently had mastered Greek, Latin, Hebrew, Arabic and other languages. Throughout his work of several thousand pages he constantly referred to texts from several languages and gave various readings and possible translations.

Two great German scholars, C. F. Keil and F. Delitzsch, whose commentary on the Old Testament occupies nearly twelve thousand pages, are held in high esteem by

LDS scholars who accept the Old Testament to be basically a divine record. Keil and Delitzsch are thought to be quite conservative and quite fundamental; yet they show a constant concern over the accuracy of the translation and transmission of the ancient texts.

In a major sense every commentary on the Bible is *prima facie* evidence that its writers and sponsors believe the Bible to be true only as far as it is translated or interpreted correctly. In a major sense every new translation is *prima facie* evidence that the translators and the church groups who support and sponsor it believe the Bible to be true only as far as it is translated and interpreted correctly. The Catholics have produced a new translation in recent times, and various Protestant groups have produced several new and supposedly improved translations since the 1930s. Some of these translations are from very liberal groups — those who tend to look upon the Bible as literature and legend. And others have come from very fundamental groups — those who tend to look upon the Bible as being absolutely true and divinely preserved and transmitted. Among this latter group is the Jehovah's Witnesses translation, which alters the King James text so much in some places as almost to be a commentary instead of a translation. The same could be said of some parts of the most liberal translations.

Of course, it is impossible to translate the Bible without interjecting some interpretation. For instance, we learn from the Prophet Joseph Smith that when Genesis 1:1 uses the plural form of the Hebrew word for God, *Eloheim*, the writer meant it literally. (*Teachings of the Prophet Joseph Smith*, comp. Joseph Fielding Smith [Salt Lake City: Deseret Book Co., 1938], page 371; hereafter cited as *TPJS*. It is interesting, however, that the Prophet did not, himself, always

translate *Eloheim* as *Gods* in the Inspired Version and the
Book of Moses, where he does a lot with this passage.) The
scholars of the world have always rendered it *God* and have
called it the "plurality of majesty." This is based on
assumption rather than revelation. That is, the translators,
for hundreds of years, have assumed that God is a single,
formless spirit that fills the immensity of space. Hence, the
translation must conform to that assumption or belief. This
is not translation; it is interpretation. This assumption is
possibly as much as seventeen hundred years old; but age
does not make it true. Nor is it proved true just because 99
percent of the Jewish and Christian scholars accept it today.
No matter how many scholars of whatever faiths accept it, it
still should be labeled for what it is—an interpretation.
Latter-day Saints should not accept this kind of authori-
tarianism; and because they usually don't, they are able to
appreciate much that the world has to skip by or explain
away. They are able to take it literally instead of interpreting it into something else. (See John 10:34, where Jesus
explains Psalm 82:6.)

What is said above is not meant to cast doubt on the
sincerity of the translators. Even those who have taken
liberties with the text have sincerely believed that they were
justified. By and large the translators have been very con-
scientious and diligent and have done a great service to
mankind. This was especially true of the King James translators, Martin Luther, and other early translators. It is
remarkable how little they interpreted in their translations.
The mischief referred to in 1 Nephi 13, whereby the plain
and precious things were taken out, apparently was perpetrated some time between about A.D. 90 and A.D. 200.
This particular attack on the Bible could not have occurred

any earlier than that, because Nephi said that the Bible would be pure when it should go forth by the hand of the apostles of Jesus (see 1 Nephi 13:24-25), which we now know took place in approximately the time span of A.D. 40 to A.D. 90. We say that the deletions must have been made by about A.D. 200 because the New Testament has been pretty well preserved since that time. So many extant texts of the New Testament go back to about 200 that we can say with reasonable assurance that it has not been robbed of "many parts which are plain and most precious" since that time. The modern New Testament record is essentially the same as that of A.D. 200.

It is possible that Nephi had reference to the Old Testament as well as the New Testament when he referred to a book from the mouth of a Jew that would go forth to the Gentiles via the apostles of the Lamb and would subsequently lose plain and precious parts. The scripture referred to and quoted by the apostles in their missionary work was, of course, the Old Testament record. While the Old Testament is a more complex problem in this regard because of the dating of the Septuagint (a Greek-language version of the Old Testament dating somewhere between 300 and 200 B.C.), there are still indications that plain and precious things may have been removed from it between the time of the apostles and A.D. 200.

One clue is that in Romans 11:15-24 Paul discusses the parable of the tame and the wild olive tree in such a manner as to suggest that he was quoting then-existent scripture. Apparently the source of this parable is Zenos. (See Jacob 5 and 6.) Zenos is one of four books mentioned in the Book of Mormon as being in the brass plates of Laban, so it seems likely that these books were included in the Bible from Jere-

miah's day on down to the apostles' day. The four books are
Zenos, Zenock, Neum and Ezias. (See, for example, 1
Nephi 19:10 and Helaman 8:20.)

In order for the "most abominable church" mentioned
by Nephi to have been successful in doing what Nephi said it
would do to the Bible, presumably there must have been
some cooperation between the Jews and apostate Christians.
There would have had to be a great deal of destruction of
texts, wherever those texts might have been housed. We
know that the priesthood was gone and the apostasy complete by the year 200. The church that emerged was
increasingly apostate, even allowing for good intentions.
That records were altered to suit apostate beliefs is not a far-
fetched supposition by any means. (Modern communist
governments have more than once "rewritten history" with
similar objectives.)

The reason why we can be sure that the apostasy had
occurred by the year 200 is that by then the apostles (except
John, who was not functioning to sustain a doomed church)
had been dead for a hundred years or more. The keys being
gone, the Church could not be perpetuated. A bishop
cannot ordain his successor, for example, and he cannot
ordain an apostle. There is a limit to how long the true
Church can be perpetuated in any form if all of the General
Authorities are gone. It is true that the various offices of the
Melchizedek Priesthood have certain keys and prerogatives
that might be used under heavenly direction to reorganize
the Church; but there is no evidence that anything like that
was done during the second century. In fact, quite the opposite. From an LDS point of view we would have to say that,
whatever happened, it was of a disorganizing rather than an
organizing character.

There is evidence that an apostate group was already in operation in the Church in New Testament times. John spoke of anti-Christs in the Church. (See 2 John 2:18-19; 1 John 4:1-3; 2 John 1:7.) His description shows that they were Gnostics. The Nicolaitans of Revelation 3:6 were of this same persuasion. Paul too spoke of apostasy, using such names as "son of perdition," "that Wicked," and "the mystery of iniquity" that already was at work. (See 2 Thessalonians 2:1-12.) With reference to how long the true leaders could hold out, he said, "Only he who now letteth [prevents or holds back] will let until they are taken out of the way." In other words, that living generation of General Authorities would be all that would stand in the way of the success of the apostate church. This is further emphasized in 2 Corinthians. This whole epistle was written to dissuade the Saints at Corinth from following the apostates in the Church of Christ who were trying to lead them astray. (See especially chapters 11 and 12.)

While the Bible has remained relatively unchanged since about A.D. 200, and while the translators—at least of earlier versions, such as the King James—have done a very creditable job, there has been another influence at work undermining the Bible's reputation as the word of God. This influence goes by the prestigious title of "higher criticism." Its roots go back a long way, but it did not have any significant effect on popular acceptance of the Bible until the rise of the modern theories and studies on the origin of man. Such studies led to the assumption that the existence of primitive beings gives credence to the idea of primitive religion.

Latter-day Saints, of course, know that Adam and Eve, the parents of all living, were perfect in human form and, before the Fall, immortal. Their perfection probably went beyond physical things. They were among the most excellent of our Heavenly Father's spirit children. Unlike other Christians, Latter-day Saints hold them in very high regard and also understand that they were taught by the Lord. Their learning may have exceeded that of modern men in certain ways. Generations later, Abraham apparently had a knowledge of astronomy and mathematics superior to that of anyone in the last two or three thousand years. It is not clear that modern man has yet caught up with him. It may well be that knowledge of this kind had been handed down from the patriarchs before him. Of course, Abraham received some of it directly from the Lord, but there is no reason to reject the idea that early patriarchs had similar knowledge.

Since the days of the ancient patriarchs, in many respects man has spiritually and physically regressed rather than progressed. The long life-span of the antedeluvians has been confirmed by modern revelation. Life expectancy from the standpoint of an actuarial table has increased over the past century, but real life expectancy in the sense of true potential longevity has decreased since the time of the Flood. Of course, spiritual and secular knowledge have ebbed and flowed throughout the ages. There have been great dispensations of the gospel, partial dispensations, and periods of darkness and apostasy. But the concept of a gradual evolution of religion from primitive to enlightened forms is not an accurate description of what happened.

Some higher critics also use assumptions that grow out of their studies and theories in seeking to determine the age of the books of the Old Testament. For instance, they consider certain ideas ''primitive'' and others more "advanced." If a book has "primitive" ideas in it, it is given an earlier date than if it contains more "advanced" ideas. The idea that God has a body is considered primitive. The concept is called anthropomorphism—from *anthropo* (manlike) and *morphe* (form)—meaning, in the form of man. Also, the idea that there is more than one god, called polytheism, is labeled a primitive concept. Many higher critics believe that the Jews gave up polytheism and anthropomorphism at a fairly early date—at least by the time of Ezra after the Babylonian captivity. In fact, most think that Moses was a monotheist (believer in only one god). The following statement from the *Encyclopedia Judaica* not only shows how these beliefs have affected higher criticism, but also hints at some of the problems they produce:

> Anthropomorphism is a normal phenomenon in all primitive and ancient polytheistic religions. In Jewish literary sources from the Bible to the *aggadah* and Midrashim, the use of anthropomorphic descriptions and expressions (both physical and psychical) is also widespread. Yet at the same time it is accepted as a major axiom of Judaism, from the biblical period onward, that no material representation of the Deity is possible or permissible. The resolution of this apparent contradiction requires consideration and understanding of virtually every anthropomorphic expression. In every instance it should be asked whether the expression is an actual, naively concrete personification of God, or a fresh and vital form of religious awareness resorting to corporeal imagery, or an allegorical expression, in which the anthropomorphism is not merely an aesthetic means for the shaping of a particular perception or utterance, but is rather a conscious method of artificially clothing spiritual contents in concrete imagery.
>
> The evolutionary approach to the study of religion, which mainly developed in the nineteenth century, sug-

gested a line of development beginning with anthropomorphic concepts and leading up to a more purified spiritual
faith. It argued, among other things, that corporeal repre-
sentations of the Deity were more commonly found in the
older portions of the Bible than in its later books. This view
does not distinguish between the different possible explanations for anthropomorphic terms. It especially fails to
account for the phenomenon common in the history of all
cultures, that sometimes a later period can be more primitive than an earlier one. In fact, both personifications of
the Deity as well as attempts to avoid them are found side
by side in all parts of the Bible. The paucity of anthropo-
morphisms in certain works is not necessarily proof of any
development in religion, but may well be due to the literary
characteristics and intentions of certain biblical narratives,
e.g., the narratives designed to express the growing distance
between God and man through describing His relationship
to Adam, the patriarchs, and the early and late prophets,
etc. (*Encyclopedia Judaica*, 16 vols., s.v. "Anthropomorphism" [Keter Publishing House Jerusalem Ltd., 1972].)

Among other things, take note that the foregoing
excerpt shows that such critics have taken on an impossible
task: that of analyzing every biblical passage about Deity
and determining in each case whether it is a primitive
reference to a god in human form, an allegorical reference
to a god in human form, a primitive idea in a late period, a
late idea in a primitive period, and so forth. Latter-day
Saints don't have to go through all these mental gymnastics,
because they know the true doctrine of Deity. They have
modern prophets who have seen God and have heard his
voice. They know that Jesus was resurrected, because their
prophets have seen him and have borne witness of him over
and over again. They have new revelations which support
and defend the Bible. They have descriptions of God's

power, glory and intelligence that overcome all of the philosophical problems invented by an unenlightened scholarship. They know that God can and does have a body in the same form as man's, composed of material substance, and that this body dwells on a planet near Kolob in the midst of everlasting burnings. They know that his influence is omnipresent by the power of his Spirit—which, no doubt, is the "televising" power of heavenly beings.

One of the assumptions of higher critics is that a prophet cannot foretell. Hence, when Isaiah names Cyrus (Isaiah 44:28; 45:1) as the deliverer of the Jews from captivity, they assume that a later person, a "deutero" or second Isaiah—someone who lived after Cyrus—wrote this part of Isaiah. Thus, the *Encyclopedia Judaica* article on Isaiah refers to this repeatedly as evidence to support a Second Isaiah or Deutero-Isaiah. The article, among other things, says: "The virtually unanimous opinion in modern times is that Isaiah is to be considered the work of two distinct authors. . . . The dramatic turn of events of his time, the impending conquest of Babylonia by Cyrus, the Persian King of Elam (539 B.C.E.), to which the prophet alludes . . . enables the prophet's utterances to be dated with approximate accuracy to 540 B.C.E." (*Encyclopedia Judaica*, s.v. "Isaiah.") This, of course, casts doubt on the integrity of the prophets or the original authors of the Bible and on the value of the Bible as an inspired authority. Some of the higher critics are, themselves, quite devout; but apostasy and infidelity follow them wherever they go.

There are four main areas of Old Testament thought and authority on which higher criticism has cast doubt. They are: the authorship of the five books of Moses; the authorship of Isaiah (who foretold so many details of the life of Jesus and of the Restoration); the Old Testament witness of Christ; and the reality of the miracles and catastrophic events. It is interesting that the Book of Mormon comes to the Bible's rescue in each of these areas.

The higher critics cast doubt on the books of Moses by ascribing them to a much later date than Moses' time and by saying that they are a compilation of myths from primitive peoples. But it is clear from the Book of Mormon that Moses really was the author of, at least, most of the Pentateuch, and Isaiah was the author of both halves of the book which bears his name. The Book of Mormon quotes from the so-called First Isaiah and the so-called Deutero-Isaiah and gives credit to Isaiah for all. Also, we know that the Book of Mormon prophets' copy of Isaiah came with them to America in 600 B.C., long before so-called Deutero-Isaiah supposedly lived and wrote. And, of course, the important miracles and cataclysms are mentioned in the Book of Mormon. The whole Book of Mormon is a witness of the divinity of Jesus Christ. (See chapter six for further discussion and documentation on this subject.)

It can be seen from the foregoing that higher criticism may have the effect of destroying the Bible as an authoritative source of theology and even of conduct. For if the Bible does not tell the truth about theology (the nature of God, man, the eternal worlds, etc.) and history (the Fall, the Flood, the division of the continents, the Exodus, etc.), why should we believe it tells the truth about moral and ethical law? It is one thing if Moses is the author of the Ten Commandments; it is another thing if God is. It is one thing if it really was the Red Sea that was divided; it is another if the Israelites waded across a marsh from which the waters had receded due to a strong wind.

Every reader of the Bible will approach it from some bias. The bias of a true Latter-day Saint is that it is basically the word of God. The bias of a higher critic (a category which embraces the majority of the Christian scholars of our day) is that the prophets were smart men who recognized that their thoughts were revolutionary and brilliant — maybe even true, and at the very least progressive. One of these scholars said that the difference between an Isaiah and somebody whose thoughts perished in the rubble of antiquity was that an Isaiah had the courage to call himself a prophet and claim that he spoke for God. The true followers of the Savior know that Isaiah saw God and was called by him. They know that, when he wrote them, his words were true. If the words attributed to him are any less true today, it is not because the world has changed, but only because some of his words may have been changed or lost.

Thus the official position of The Church of Jesus Christ of Latter-day Saints is that the Bible is true as far as it is translated correctly. In this context, however, *translated* probably comes closer to meaning transmitted than translated. True, there are errors due to translation and to interpretation in the process of translation. Also many parts are missing, and probably there are some copying problems as well. Nevertheless, we rightly assume the truth of the Bible unless we can show that it is in error in specific places. We are cautious about biblical teachings that are not verified by modern revelation or that appear only once in the Bible and seem out of place or out of harmony with the rest of the Bible. But we understand more of the Bible and cherish its teachings more than does any other church.

In instances wherein an error exists in the Bible, there are two methods of discovering it. The first is modern

revelation. In the main this method is confined to Joseph
Smith's inspired "translation" of the Bible, which was not
a translation in the accepted sense but a restoration by
revelation of the original thought or wording. The whole
book of Moses in the Pearl of Great Price is an example of
the "translation" work that Joseph Smith did. It is a restoration of the early chapters of Genesis. Also in the Pearl of
Great Price we find the inspired translation of Matthew 24.
The whole Inspired Version of the Bible contains many
corrections made by the Prophet Joseph Smith. His main
tool was revelation—all the way from great and profound
communications, such as would account for Moses 1, to the
whisperings of the Spirit, which would explain John 4:24.
He also studied languages. He was a quick learner and
picked up some German and Hebrew. This knowledge was
primarily helpful to him as it triggered the Spirit into
greater activity. He never approached the linguistic ability
necessary to translate Hebrew or Greek texts such as those
used in Bible translations.

The second method of discovering errors in the Bible
is, of course, scholarship. This is a work that is going on and
will go on. But scholarship has to be scrutinized and tested
over long periods of time. One problem with it is that, if the
texts are in error, the scholarship may only compound
rather than correct the error. Another is that unless the
scholars assume that the Bible is inspired they will not treat
it with the respect it deserves. When dealing with scholarly
criticism, the Latter-day Saint should learn to deduce the
biases of the writer and also should inquire into his creden-
tials. It is one thing if the scholar is fundamental (a strong
believer and devout respecter of the Bible) in his approach
and does not pretend to be going beyond his own language

and the prophets. It is another thing if he takes a pseudo-scientific stance and, in addition, pretends to be able to deal with the languages without the profound knowledge required in this work. A good listener or reader can learn to distinguish between good and bad scholarship if he is willing to struggle with it and practice quiet forbearance and healthy skepticism until he knows that he knows.

One of the hazards we face in discussing the possibility of errors of translation or transmission is that we may sound too skeptical. We may appear to question or cast doubt on the value of studying the book. That would be a tragedy, because the Old Testament just might have more down-to-earth practical value for everyday living than any other book. It is a terribly frank book, a book of surprising honesty. It hides or excuses no human faults. In reading it we see not only the greatness of the prophets but also their weaknesses.

We see, too, that the Lord always sustained his prophets. He never countenanced rebellion against them. One gets the impression that, even if the prophets were wrong, the Lord would not take some rebel and say to him: "Moses is a fallen prophet. I am going to start over with you. You go away and set up a new church called 'The Church of the Firstborn' [for example], and let the world know that you are taking over, that you are getting things straightened out and back on the right course."

When the chosen people started to stray, he would warn them through their constituted and sustained leaders. Then, if they insisted on pursuing their folly—as did Israel when it insisted on having a king—he would let them do so. Only there would be a change in the structure of their covenant. He would start over with the same group and the same leaders. All of them would be offered a new covenant with less blessings available through it, but an opportunity to be restored back to the old and more complete covenant. But he changed his leaders only through death of the old ones, and the new ones were publicly sustained. Nothing was done in a corner. This and a thousand other lessons that bear on real life and real problems are in the Old Testament, to be found by those who diligently seek them. And that is why the Old Testament just might be the ''first book as well as the last.''

2

A Short History of the Old Testament Canon

The Christian and Jewish worlds in general believe that the Old Testament started as myth and gradually evolved into something like its present form in the last few centuries before the Christian era. But the Latterday Saints know better than this. The Lord restored a part of the book of Genesis lost long ago—the book of Moses. From it we learn that Adam recorded the word of God in a "book of remembrance" and taught his children to read and write. (See Moses 6:5-6.)

The Lord, by his own finger, gave the pattern for the writing of the first scriptures (Moses 6:46) and has, from that time forth, commanded that accurate records be kept of his dealings with mankind (see, for example, 3 Nephi 23:7-13). During each priesthood dispensation through the

earth's history, the practice of recording and preserving
God's revelations has continued. Due to neglect and deliberate destruction, many of these writings have been lost over
thousands of years. Good men have succeeded in preserving some of them, however. Because of the wickedness
of men, other writings were deliberately hidden by the
Lord so they might come forth in their purity when he
desired. (See D&C 6:26-27; 1 Nephi 13:35-41; 2 Nephi
29:1-13.)

There is one fact we cannot lose sight of, however: The
Bible has come forth essentially as God has intended it to
be. Admittedly, there are plain and precious parts which
have been removed and there has been some corruption
of the text (1 Nephi 13:26-27); nevertheless, the book has
been miraculously preserved and is still sufficiently pure and
powerful to stand as a divinely recognized witness for Christ
which has blessed millions of lives both in and out of the
Church of Jesus Christ.

This is not to say that all of the prophets realized their
writings would become part of a large volume of scripture.
Some, such as Moses, formalized their writings into a collection; but the idea that these would be joined to other
writings to form a single large book is rarely evidenced in
their works. God intended this to be the case, however. It is
interesting that, as he inspired Nephi to make a second and
more religious history of his people, Nephi was left to
wonder as to its purpose (1 Nephi 9:5-6), as was Mormon,
who stated that he included Nephi's writings in his record
because of the whisperings of the Spirit (Words of Mormon
1:6-7). God does not always reveal all his purposes to his
prophets. Nevertheless, he knows the end from the beginning and reaches his own ends. Therefore, when the scribe
Ezra (ca. 520 B.C.), according to tradition, brought together

all the sacred writings which had been preserved by the Jews, carefully examined them and then selected those which were deemed authentic and placed them in a formal canon as the forerunner of our Old Testament, he was acting under inspiration much as did Mormon on the American continent. Once these holy materials were brought together, not only were they more easily preserved but also more readily copied, thus making them more available for instruction to the people.

DIVISIONS IN THE OLD TESTAMENT

The Old Testament can be divided into four major divisions. The first contains the writings of Moses: Genesis, Exodus, Leviticus, Numbers and Deuteronomy. This section is sometimes referred to as the Pentateuch, a Greek title that, roughly translated, means "five books of law." To the Jews it was known as the Torah, that is, "the Law." The next division contains the books of a more historical nature. These trace the dealings of God with the covenant people from the days of Joshua to the Jews' return from the Babylonian exile. Therefore, these books are referred to collectively as "the history." They include the books from Joshua through Esther. The works of poets and sages comprise the next division known as "the wisdom literature" and includes the works from Job to the Song of Solomon. (Joseph Smith said that the Song of Solomon should not be in the Old Testament in spite of its poetic quality.) The last division, from Isaiah to Malachi, is known as "the prophets" and is subdivided into two sections: the major prophets, consisting of Isaiah, Jeremiah, Lamentations (written by Jeremiah), Ezekiel, and Daniel; and the minor prophets from Hosea to Malachi.

THE OLD TESTAMENT IS AN INSPIRED RECORD

The eighth article of faith reads, in part: "We believe the Bible to be the word of God as far as it is translated correctly." Is it possible to find all of the errors and correct them? Probably not; but there are valid and useful methods of detecting errors. Careful scholarship over long periods of time is of some value. The Inspired Version, the Inspired Translation of Joseph Smith, is of great value. The other standard works of the Church give many keys. The Book of Mormon is especially valuable in this regard because it reveals in purity the doctrines which were understood by the faithful Saints in the Old Testament times. Therefore, by using the modern scriptures as a guide, the Bible can be approached with confidence.

The admission that there are mistakes of translation in the Bible should not be taken to mean that there are great portions of the Old Testament in error. According to the Book of Mormon, the major reason the Bible became a stumbling block to the Gentiles was that plain and precious truths were removed from it by a church which was more abominable than any other church. (See 1 Nephi 13:23-29.) Therefore, the biggest problem with the Old Testament is not as much textual corruptions as it is deletions.

The Lord has restored some of those plain and precious portions in this day. This was a major purpose for the preservation and eventual translation of the Book of Mormon. Therefore, the Bible and the Book of Mormon complement and complete one another. (See 1 Nephi 13:40-41.) Thus, Ezekiel saw that the record of Judah (the Bible) and the record of Joseph (the Book of Mormon) would be joined, "and they shall become one" in the hand of Ephraim (Ezekiel 37:15-17). For this reason God could tell his church to "teach the principles of my gospel, which are in the Bible and the Book of Mormon, in the which is the fulness of the gospel" (D&C 42:12).

In spite of its limitations, the Bible is an inspired work of great purity and beauty. The Lord's hand has been at work in preserving this sacred volume. He has done it in such a way that a great many of its truths have been retained. An understanding of how the Lord has done this is not only interesting but will provide a major key in understanding the Old Testament. The apostle Paul elucidated the basic principle. He wrote:

> For what man knoweth the things of a man, save the spirit of man which is in him? even so the things of God knoweth no man, but the Spirit of God.
>
> Now we have received, not the spirit of the world, but the spirit which is of God; that we might know the things that are freely given to us of God.
>
> Which things also we speak, not in the words which man's wisdom teacheth, but which the Holy Ghost teacheth; comparing spiritual things with spiritual.
>
> But the natural man receiveth not the things of the Spirit of God: for they are foolishness unto him: neither can he know them, because they are spiritually discerned. (1 Corinthians 2:11-14.)

This makes it possible for the Lord to conceal his teachings from the corrupt and perverse. The apostle Paul used the word *mystery* to describe teachings handled this way (see, for example, Ephesians 1:9; 3:1-10; Colossians 1:26; 1 Timothy 3:16), but he stressed that such things were not hidden from the Saints:

> Now to him that is of power to stablish you according to my gospel, and the preaching of Jesus Christ, according to the revelation of the mystery, which was kept secret since the world began,

> But now is made manifest, and by the scriptures of the
> prophets, according to the commandment of the everlasting
> God, made known to all nations for the obedience of faith.
> . . . (Romans 16:25-26; see also 1 Corinthians 2:6-10.)

Note that Paul states that the "mysteries" were made
manifest "by the scriptures of the prophets." The scriptures
to which he referred were those of the Old Testament. He
knew that the person who would approach that work by the
Spirit would find the "revelation of the mystery." Thus he
could say to Timothy, "the holy scriptures [i.e., the Old
Testament] are able to make thee wise unto salvation" (2
Timothy 3:15). It was by the locking of his word behind the
spirit of revelation that the Lord protected it from the
corrupt hands of the ungodly and at the same time retained
within it sufficient power to lift those who were moved by
the Spirit.

The apostle Peter wrote, "For the prophecy came not
in old time by the will of man: but holy men of God spake as
they were moved by the Holy Ghost" (2 Peter 1:21). We
now turn our attention to look briefly at the writings of these
ancient holy men. As we do so, it should be kept in mind
that, as Peter said, they spoke by the power of the Holy
Ghost. Emphasizing the implications of this fact the prophet
Nephi explained:

> Do ye not remember that I said unto you that after ye
> had received the Holy Ghost ye could speak with the tongue
> of angels? And now, how could ye speak with the tongue
> of angels save it were by the Holy Ghost?
> Angels speak by the power of the Holy Ghost; wherefore,
> they speak the words of Christ. Wherefore, I said unto you,
> feast upon the words of Christ; for behold, the words of

Christ will tell you all things what ye should do. (2 Nephi 32:2-3.)

Thus, the ancients spoke the words of Christ and in so doing were able to capture his Spirit. (Bear in mind that the brass plates which Nephi used were a pure form of the Old Testament. He quoted Isaiah the most, and Isaiah was not changed very much.)

THE WRITINGS OF MOSES

The first author whose work is recorded in the Bible is Moses. Whether or not he had access to more ancient writings which were preserved through the Flood and added to by other prophets from Noah to Joseph is unknown to worldly scholars. Certainly writings of Abraham and Joseph were extant in Moses' day for these were preserved among the Egyptians and later came into the hands of Joseph Smith. (See Joseph Smith, Jr., *History of the Church of Jesus Christ of Latter-day Saints,* ed. B. H. Roberts, 7 vols. [Salt Lake City: The Church of Jesus Christ of Latter-day Saints, 1949], 2:236; hereafter cited as *HC.*) The Book of Mormon makes it plain that the Hebrew scriptures in 600 B.C. contained extensive writings and prophecies of Joseph which have since been lost. (See 2 Nephi 4:1-2; and Inspired Version, Genesis 48ff.) This could be an indication that his writings were preserved and placed into the collections of sacred works. Whatever the case, Moses received much of his knowledge through revelation, from which he knew of the Creation and the Fall as well as the ministry of Enoch. (See, for example, Moses 1:1-2; 2:1.) Thus, revelation appears to be a major source of his record.

Genesis

The name *Genesis* is derived from the ancient Greek version of the Bible called the Septuagint. *Genesis* means "origin." In the Hebrew Bible, following the practice of denoting a book from the first important word which it contained, it is called "in the beginning." This title is very apt, since the book contains the most ancient of histories. Through its pages unfolds the story of the divine Creation, the Fall of man, the initial peopling of the earth, and the spread of the greatest righteousness and greatest evil ever achieved by man. The righteousness led to the building and eventual translation of Enoch's "city of holiness," while the evil brought on the universal Flood. The book tells of the re-establishment of the covenant, originally made with Adam and his righteous posterity, with Abraham, Isaac, and Jacob, and it traces the beginnings of God's chosen people.

It is interesting that this one book, which comprises no more than 5 percent of the total volume of the Bible, covers over 50 percent of its time span, nearly twenty-five hundred years. This means that Moses was one thousand years closer to Christ than to Adam. The contents of Genesis are merely highlights of important events. Those events, however, carefully chosen by the great historian, give us an important understanding about God and his dealings with man.

Exodus

The name given to the second book of Moses by the writers of the Septuagint was derived from the greatest event chronicled in the book. The Greek word *exodus* means "going out" or "departing." In the Hebrew Bible it is called "these are the names," since those are the words with which it begins.

Exodus picks up where Genesis leaves off. It tells of the death of Joseph and the growth into a mighty people of the seventy souls who followed Jacob into Egypt. It explains why they were placed in captivity and why Pharaoh eventually ordered the death of all Israelite male babies. How Moses escaped this decree and was raised by his mother in the Pharaoh's house as a son of an Egyptian princess is also told. At the age of forty, Moses threw in his lot with the Hebrews and was forced to flee the land. His meeting with Jethro, his marriage, and his eventual call from God (at the age of eighty) are all recounted.

The high point of the book concentrates on the great display of divine power used to assist the Israelites in their escape from Egypt, and Jehovah's offer to renew his full covenant with them. Indeed, the book reveals the greatest direct intervention by the Lord in the affairs of men this side of the great Flood. Though he would again and again display his power to ancient Israel, it would never be as direct nor as constant as at that time. Moses was enabled to bring plague after plague upon all the land of Egypt in his attempt to teach Pharaoh that the Hebrew deity was indeed God and that Pharaoh must free Israel that they might worship God. During all this time of great suffering in the area inhabited by the Egyptians, the Israelite area of Goshen seems to have been continually spared. Eventually, Moses was able to free Israel, only to find Pharaoh had gone against his word and sent his army to destroy them. This led to the parting of the Red Sea through which Israel escaped and in which Pharaoh's army drowned.

This was not the end of the display of divine power. In the wilderness the Lord directed the travels of Israel with a pillar of fire by night and a cloud by day. Eventually he

brought them to his holy mountain and there gave Moses
the law by which Israel could become his people. There
Moses attempted to prepare the people to meet Jehovah, but
the people would not, turning to idolatry instead. Their
subsequent wandering for forty years in the wilderness is
recorded, emphasizing Jehovah's further assistance to them
by providing quail, manna, and water. Over and over one is
impressed with the long-suffering of the Lord and his
prophet. Because of these things, it is of little wonder that
Jews and Christians alike have looked back on these never-
since-repeated days as evidence of the Lord's love and
omnipotence. There will come another day, however, in the
not-too-distant future when Jehovah will once again display
such power. So great will that display be that men will no
longer refer to the days of Moses, but to this greater day
when the Lord will again make bare his arm before the
nations. (See Jeremiah 16:14-15.)

In addition to the revelation of the power of Jehovah,
Moses recorded the laws, statutes, and ordinances which he
received by revelation for the salvation of Israel. Chief
among these was the Ten Commandments. In addition, he
recorded the instructions for building the tabernacle and
preparing its furnishings as well as the nature of the dress of
the priests. He also recorded the eventual erection and consecration of the tabernacle and the grand display of glory by
which it was divinely approved. Finally, Moses recounted
Israel's journey while being led by the divine pillar.

Leviticus

The Septuagint called the third book of Moses "Leviticus" after the Levites, while in the Hebrew Bible it is known
as "and he called." The most appropriate name is that by

which the book is called in the Jewish Mishnah: "The Priest's Manual." Exodus dealt with the giving of the law and the building and erection of the tabernacle. Leviticus deals with the implementation of the law through the ministration of the priests after the order of Aaron, and it describes how the tabernacle and its furnishings were to be used for worship. Since all of this was the special prerogative of the priests of the Aaronic Priesthood, the duties of the lesser Levites are not catalogued in this book but are given in the book of Numbers. Both the priests and the Levites were of the tribe of Levi.

Though Leviticus focused primarily upon the priests, few of the laws recorded therein pertain exclusively to them. Rather, the law was defined in such a way as to allow them to administer and teach it to the people. For this reason it could be considered a technical manual or handbook of instructions for the priests. Its primary emphasis was to help them distinguish the difference between holy and unholy, and between clean and unclean: "And that ye may teach the children of Israel all the statutes which the Lord hath spoken unto them by the hand of Moses" (Leviticus 10:11). This emphasis makes the real burden of the book clear. God is holy; therefore, he cannot dwell in unholy temples nor among unholy people, nor, for that matter, they with him. (See Moses 6:57; D&C 97:17.) The charge to the priest was, then, twofold: to teach the people how to be holy, and to cleanse the people and the sanctuary when they were defiled.

In this book Moses recorded the ordinances of sacrifice and offerings by which Israel could renew and continue in their covenant relationship with Jehovah. Next he described the inauguration of the services of the tabernacle through which the ordinances were administered. This was followed by the laws by which impurities of body, home, and sanctuary could be detected and cleansed. (In this respect it is interesting to note that when an object became unclean, such as mildew or rot in a garment, total destruction was unnecessary. Only the affected portion was destroyed, leaving the good portion free for reuse.) Next, Moses treated the proper preparation of foods, the importance of holiness, and those things which would make a priest unfit to serve. Finally, with an intervening section on miscellanea, he discussed the holy days or festivals and the Sabbatical and Jubilee years. The final chapter tells how items were to be dedicated to God and his service.

Numbers

The name of the fourth book of Moses comes from the account of the marshalling and numbering of the Israelites during their circuitous travels to the Holy Land. The title appropriately applies only to chapters one, two, three, and twenty-six. In traditional Hebrew Bibles it carries the more descriptive title "in the wilderness."

Though there are a number of places where the accounts in Exodus and Numbers come together, Numbers emphasizes something which is more obscure in Exodus: Before God established his covenant with the Israelites at Sinai their lack of faith was not punished; after Sinai, it was. Israel's repeated failures and chastisements by God, though depressing in and of themselves, do leave at least one message of consolation: Jehovah is shown to be a God of grace and mercy who repeatedly offers to Israel another chance to live the covenant.

The book can be divided into three main sections. The first deals with the last nineteen days of Israel's stay at Sinai.

Here is recorded the method used to number and organize the Israelites for their marches and how the Levites were separated out and prepared for their duties. Various ordinances are also detailed.

The second section covers the next thirty-eight years, from the departure from Sinai to the encampment on the Jordanian highlands across from Jericho. This period of travel was necessary because of rebellion. It placed Israel in a position wherein they could prove themselves to God and develop faith and trust in him. While in the wilderness they were totally dependent on Jehovah for everything: food, water, clothing, shelter, and guidance. Not once were they disappointed. Continually the Lord proved himself, even to the display of obvious miracles. Yet Israel developed neither faith nor trust. Contention, rebellion and insurrection mark the history of the older generation that Jehovah brought out of Egypt. It is little wonder God would not allow such a people to possess the promised land.

The last section of the history records the events which took place on the steppes of Moab. The unsuccessful attempt of Balak, the Moabite king, and Balaam, a sorcerer, to use the power of Jehovah to defeat Israel is recounted. Also, some attention is given to the destruction of the land once Israel had secured the area, to the circumstances under which women were to have the right to inherit property, and to various festival sacrifices and vows.

Deuteronomy

The name of the last book of Moses was borrowed from the Latin Vulgate version of the scriptures, which no doubt borrowed it from the Greek Septuagint. The word translates "second law" or "the repeated law." The Hebrew Bible entitles it "these are the words," following their custom of using the first significant words of the text. The word chosen for the Greek and Latin version is quite appropriate, since the book repeats both law and history already recorded. It is not a mere repetition, however. As Leviticus was for the priests and Numbers for the Levites, so Deuteronomy is for the people. Therefore, while it is not so detailed nor technical as the books which precede it, it contains all the essential elements which the individual must obey to insure the continual blessings associated with the covenant life.

Much of the book is a series of addresses delivered by Moses to Israel as they prepared to enter the promised land. There is an urgency in Deuteronomy as Moses pleads with the people to remember God and live his law. This urgency is understandable, not only because of what Israel was about to do, but also because of Moses' knowledge that he would very soon be taken from them. His message is one of warning, hope, and reminiscence.

Deuteronomy covers a wide range of topics. Moses' first discourse was about the journeys of Israel, stressing the continual operation of the hand of God in their behalf. His next discourse was on the Ten Commandments, with a lengthy concentration on the first commandment and a look at special laws and statutes designed to supplement the Decalogue. These can be subdivided into three areas: ceremonial laws, civil laws, and criminal laws. The next section treats miscellaneous laws apparently arranged in no particular order. Then Moses instructed the people to erect an altar on Mt. Gerizim and on Mt. Ebal, both located in the Holy Land, and he told them to write the blessings for obedience on the former and the cursings for transgression on the latter. Moses then appealed to the people to be obedient so that the curses would not befall them. Finally, the book recounts the appointment of Joshua, Moses' final blessing upon the people, and his supposed death on Mt. Nebo. This last was probably the work of a later editor who put the book in its present form.

That Moses would give the law a second time seems only natural. All of the older generation but Caleb and Joshua had died in the desert. The new generation, whose privilege it would be to obtain the Holy Land, deserved to hear it as their fathers had heard it. All that had gone before was forgiven. Whatever occurred thereafter would be up to them. If they learned from the past, the future would be void of the tragedies which befell their ancestors. If not, the future would be no better.

THE HISTORICAL BOOKS

The books in this section are primarily historical narrative written in such a way as to expose the hand of God in the affairs of the nations. Taken together, these works trace a nearly continuous history from the entrance of Israel into the promised land (around 1400 B.C.) to the reestablishment of the Jews under the Persian emperor Cyrus and the rebuilding and cleansing of the temple about 400 B.C.

Joshua

The book of Joshua completed the story of the conquest of Canaan begun by Moses. There is some debate as to the author of this work. Those who deny Joshua's authorship point to a number of internal evidences such as the migration of the Danites to upper Palestine (19:47), the conquest of Caleb and Othniel that occurred after Joshua's time (15:14-19), and the recurrent statement throughout the book "unto this day" (4:9; 7:26; 8:28; 9:27; 14:14; 15:63; 16:10), which they feel reflects a definite lapse between the event and when it was recorded.

Those who insist that it is all the work of Joshua believe they are justified by the statement in 24:26: "And Joshua wrote these words in the book of the law of God." This passage, however, referred only to the recording of certain covenants made between Israel and the Lord. It is apparent that the book came to its final form after the death of Joshua but before the time of the kings of Israel. But the writer recorded those kinds of particulars which only an eyewitness would know. Therefore, it would seem that the original composition was Joshua's. Probably he recorded the events of his administration, following the example of Moses, and later this material was edited by one of the prophets (who many feel was Samuel) and placed with other holy works. (Clarke, 2:2-3.)

Joshua was an Ephraimite. He was originally called Oshea (Numbers 13:16), meaning "saved," "savior," or "salvation." But Moses changed his name to Joshua, meaning "he shall save" or "the salvation of Jehovah." The name *Jesus* is the Greek translation of Joshua. (See Acts 7:45; Hebrews 4:8.)

Shortly after the Exodus, Joshua's righteousness and leadership brought him to the fore. During the wandering of Israel, he was closely associated with Moses, whom he held in highest esteem. It was he who went up on the mount with Moses and faithfully waited the forty days for Moses to descend with the word of God. He commanded the army in the war with the Amalekites. As the prince of the tribe of Ephraim he was sent to spy upon the Holy Land in preparation for Israel's invasion. He and Caleb expressed faith that Israel could take the promised land, though the other ten princes of the tribes of Israel objected. He and Caleb were preserved, and the other ten died before Israel entered the promised land. Joshua succeeded Moses as the prophet, judge, and military commander of all Israel.

The book of Joshua can be divided into four parts. The first tells of the crossing of the Jordan and the conquest of Canaan. The second deals with the allotment of land to the tribes, including cities of refuge, as well as Levitical cities. The third section records the return home of the tribes who had an inheritance east of the Jordan. The final section reviews Joshua's last days and his burial.

As one reads the book of Joshua, he is struck with the evidence it provides of God's faithfulness to his covenants and the explanation it gives for God's purpose for the nation of Israel, as well as an explanation for why the Israelites never realized that purpose. The book clearly vindicates the Lord, showing that these people never achieved the spiritual heights in faith, obedience, and purity which the covenant people could be expected to reach.

Judges

Between the death of Joshua and the appointment of Saul as king, Israel was ruled by judges. The exploits of some of these rulers are recorded in the book bearing that title. There the term *judge* does not mean what we mean by *judge* today. These judges were appointed rulers who could administer justice, make war or peace, and lead armies. It is generally believed that they were not chosen by the people; and they were not hereditary rulers. The Bible (which may be incomplete in this area) indicates that they were chosen and raised up by God as the need arose. They had no power to make or change the laws but only to execute them under God's direction. As long as there were judges, God was the king of Israel. A possibility exists that the rule of the judges among the Nephites was patterned after the rule of the judges in Palestine—in which case elections may have been held in Palestine during times of righteousness.

Though some of the judges held wide sway, it seems apparent from the record that there were none who actually ruled over the whole land at one time. Instead, they seem to have been local figures directing and fighting together with one or two tribes. A set chronology for the book of Judges is difficult, if not impossible, to construct. All attempts to do so to date have met with major objections. Even the editor or editors are not known, though the prophet Samuel appears as a most likely candidate, since he was the last of the judges and would have had access to the material. One must remember, however, that the book of Judges is a fragmentary and short account at best. It cannot be viewed as a complete history of the era or of the rule of the judges.

This book chronicles the completion or partial completion of the conquest of Canaan, then reports the ministries of the various rulers, and ends with the migration by the tribe of Dan to the north and the war against the Benjaminites. The book does have a common theme based on the cyclical nature of the history of these years. The cycle began with Israel forsaking the covenant and chasing after false gods. Then came oppression from foreign rulers. Israel recognized her wrong and repented, and God raised up a judge who, by various means, was able to deliver the people. After the death of the judge the people fell into idolatry again. And so it went.

Two messages come out of the history. The first is the remarkable long-suffering of God toward Israel. Though his justice is fully exposed, it is played against the backdrop of his mercy. The suffering that Israel brings upon herself is used by a loving God as a means to bring her back to him. The second message is that God is the champion of his people. It is he who plans the strategy and executes it. If he wills, one man such as Sampson is given sufficient strength to overcome the enemy singlehandedly or, as in the case of Gideon, a small army is given such strength. The point is clear: If his people are true to the covenant, he will fight their battles and they will not be, indeed cannot be, overcome. On the other hand, if they break the covenant they will be left to their own devices and suffer the consequences.

Ruth

Little beyond conjecture is known of Ruth's ancestry. She lived during the time of the judges, but the exact time is uncertain. Also, it is not known how the book came into existence. Most experts think, however, that its final form is postexilic (after the Babylonian captivity) and, therefore, probably the work of the same person who wrote First and Second Samuel. This seems to be a reasonable possibility because those books contain the history of David, and this book concludes with his genealogy in which Ruth has a prominent place.

The story of the book is delightful and pure. Elimelech of Bethlehem was forced by famine to take his family, consisting of his wife Naomi and his two sons, into the less plagued land of Moab. There he died. His sons married Moabite women, one of whom was Ruth. Over the course of ten years both sons died. Naomi, hearing that the famine at home had abated, decided to return. She besought her two daughters-in-law to stay in their own land but Ruth refused. If she had been converted to Israel's God, as some think, this may have been part of the reason for her refusal; in addition she had a keen desire to care for her aging mother-in-law.

After their arrival in Bethlehem, Ruth went to the fields to glean for their support. The field she chose belonged to a wealthy farmer named Boaz, who was a kinsman of Naomi's. Upon learning of Ruth's good intentions, he assisted her. When Naomi heard the news she saw a chance for a desirable marriage for her daughter-in-law and encouraged her to pursue the opportunity. Involved in this marriage to Ruth was the redemption of Naomi's deceased husband's land, which circumstances had forced her to sell. Boaz agreed to marry Ruth and to redeem the land, thus fulfilling the ancient Mosaic duty of the kinsman in "establishing the name of the dead upon his inheritance." (Ruth 4:5; Deuteronomy 25:5-6.) Through this marriage, Obed, the grandfather of David, was born.

As with other stories in the Bible, the narrative of Ruth seems to emphasize the way God works behind the scenes to accomplish his will. On the surface everything seems to move through human agents without divine interference. The events, which appear as a chain of natural occurrences, evolve from one to another to reveal themselves in the end as the outcome of God's plan. In so doing they serve as a testimony of the quiet, yet wonderful way in which God leads men toward their destinies.

First and Second Samuel

These two books were originally one. The division between the two was first introduced in the Septuagint, which called them First and Second kingdoms followed by Third and Fourth kingdoms (1 and 2 Kings). Later, the term *kingdoms* became *kings*. The Hebrew Bible entitles the books "Samuel," probably because he is the first major personality encountered. He is not the author of the material, however, for it seems to have been written much later than the events recounted. Also, there is material included which took place after Samuel died. Whoever the compiler-editor was, it is apparent that he did have access to authentic historical documents. That Samuel and others did make records is apparent from a statement in 1 Chronicles 29:29: "Now the acts of David the king, first and last, behold, they are written in the book of Samuel the seer, and in the book of Nathan the prophet, and in the book of Gad the seer." Using these memoirs, the unknown author was able to record an accurate and insightful history of the establishment of the Israelite monarchy. (*Encyclopedia Judaica*, s.v. "Samuel, book of.")

The book recounts the rise of Samuel as the last of the judges. Under his administration the Philistines were subdued and Israel was strengthened. Israel, however, desired to have a king like other nations, and so the Lord had Samuel anoint Saul, who was able to unite Israel for a time. When he relegated to himself the prerogatives of priesthood he was rejected by the Lord, and Samuel anointed the youthful David. He became known to all Israel by single-handedly destroying the gigantic Philistine champion, Goliath. Saul became insanely jealous of David over the next few years and on a number of occasions tried to have him killed. David was forced to play hide and seek, all the while gaining support and manpower in the southern part of the kingdom. Finally, Saul's sons were killed and he was

seriously wounded by the Philistines and he took his own
life. The account of his burial concludes the book of First
Samuel.

The book of Second Samuel can be divided into three
parts. The first deals with the happy commencement of
David's reign, the second with his unhappy fall and the
miserable consequences which followed, and the third with
his restoration to partial acceptance by the Lord and the re-
establishment of his kingdom. The book ends with the
details of the latter part of his reign.

Though there is a great deal of historical material, the
overriding concern of these books is to establish the national
and religious significance of Israel's decision to be governed
by mortal kings. Under the judges, Israel had only one king,
one Lord, and one law-giver: Jehovah. Under his rule men
were made free and independent in the widest sense possible. Israel's insistence upon a human and corruptible king
was, in reality, a rejection of the direct rule of the Lord.
Even so, he could still reign through these men if they
obeyed his laws and took counsel from his prophets. If they
would not, however, Israel's choice would result in the loss
of divine leadership and she would be left to her own
resources. The story of the kings points out the tragic fact
that even excellent kings can fall, thus leaving the people in
extreme jeopardy.

First and Second Kings

As mentioned in the comments on First and Second
Samuel, these two books were originally one. The authorship of the work is not even hinted at anywhere in the text,
which has led to various theories, the chief being that the
work was that of either Jeremiah, Isaiah, or Ezra. The first

two are favored by some because several chapters in the works of both prophets parallel material found in Kings. But the most common opinion is that this is the work of Ezra. (Clarke, 2:381.)

The reasons for this opinion include the following: First, the uniformity of style and flow evidences one writer. Second, the author had access to political as well as prophetic and priestly records. It appears that Judah may have been in captivity when the work was being compiled and edited. Finally, the emphasis was less on battles, secular building projects, political addresses, and more on the temple, religious worship, morals of the kings and people, and the works of the prophets. All this points to Ezra.

The two books fall naturally into four divisions: the monarchy under David and Solomon; the division of the kingdom into that of Israel and Judah; the fall of the kingdom of Israel, and the continuation of the kingdom of Judah alone; and the fall of Judah and its aftermath.

Noted within the pages of these books are the stories of Solomon, his rise to magnificence through the use of a divine spiritual gift, and his eventual fall; the division of the kingdom between the rivals Jeroboam and Rehoboam, with the relapse of the people of the Northern Kingdom into idolatry; the ministries of Elijah, Elisha, Jeremiah, and Isaiah; the continual spiritual decline of the kingdom of Israel to its lowest level under Ahab and his wife Jezebel; the fall of the Northern Kingdom to the Assyrians; the decline of the Southern Kingdom into apostasy; and the Babylonian conquest of that kingdom and the depopulation of the land.

These books illustrate the fulfillment of the word of God in the history of the Israelites. Moses had clearly and unequivocally foretold what would happen as the people obeyed or rebelled (Deuteronomy 28). Therefore fate, chance, luck—good or ill—are not a part of the narrative. God was intimately associated with all that transpired with this vascillating and weak-willed people. To illustrate, Solomon's greatness was derived from an endowment of administrative wisdom given by Deity. Through that means he was able to expand the borders of Israel, build defense cities, and rear the house of God. But in his old age he fell to idolatry, lost his divine gift, and thereby set the course for the eventual destruction of all he worked for. The rebellion of the ten tribes eventually caused them to forfeit all divine assistance, and they fell. On the other hand, the Southern Kingdom, whose decline was retarded by the occasional reign of a good king, was assisted by direct divine intervention until it, too, forfeited that privilege. The message is clear: all Israel fell when they turned from God and broke the covenant.

First and Second Chronicles

These books should not be confused with the "chronicles of kings" often mentioned in the other historical books and apparently lost ages ago. It may be that what we have in Chronicles was abridged or taken from the "chronicles of kings." As with the books of Samuel and Kings, this work was originally one book. The title of this book was derived neither from the Septuagint nor the Vulgate, but was taken from the Greek word *chronos*, meaning "time." An adequate translation would give it the meaning of "a history of times." The Hebrew title is somewhat similar: "The words of the days." The Septuagint probably gave it the most accurate title: "Of the things that were omitted." This is because the book appeared to be a supplement to Samuel and Kings. In some traditionally correct Hebrew Bibles it is the last book. Thus, it could be considered a kind of appendix. Actually, Chronicles contains little information which cannot be found in the other historical books, and large sections of the history of David described in detail in Samuel have been omitted. It does, however, add detail to affairs of state, the building of the temple, and the organization of priests and Levites for administering therein.

As with the other historical books, the author is unknown, but the weight of evidence points to Ezra again. He would have had access to the registers of the kings and prophets and could draw his narrative from these. Because of frequent reference to them in other books of the Bible, there is little doubt that such registers were in existence and carefully kept. Further evidence of the accuracy of the registers can be seen from the character of the persons assigned to compile and care for them. These fall into two classes: professional recorders and the prophets. The Bible seems to indicate that the latter carried the greater responsibility, even to the point of intimating this may have been a part of the prophets' regular office. (Clarke, 2:573.) All the following and many others are mentioned as having kept state records: Samuel, Nathan, Iddo, Jehu, Isaiah, Hosea, and Jeremiah. Ezra, as both prophet and scribe, would meet all requirements for a record keeper.

The outline of the book falls roughly into three divisions. The first is an extended but somewhat inaccurate genealogy from Adam to David. Next comes the history of the United Kingdom under David and Solomon. The final section deals with the history of the kingdom of Judah down to the decree of Cyrus the Persian, who allowed the captive Jews to return from Babylon.

The author's objective in these books is difficult to
ascertain. Their content offers some hint, however. Matters of religion such as the worship of God, the temple,
the function of priests and Levites, and state-allowed or
state-encouraged idolatry are all emphasized. At the same
time, the troubles within the royal house of David and
Solomon are passed over as though their personal lives
were tranquil and flawless. From this it would seem that
the writer's purpose was to show that idolatry and its
attendant wickedness was the major reason for the fall of
Judah. At the same time, he was creating as broad a
background as possible for the right of the Davidic line
to rule. This emphasis would fit perfectly with the desires
Ezra might have as the Jews began again to possess their
homeland. The emphasis on the duties of priests and Levites would help push the work of the rebuilding and
rededication of the temple; the undisputed right of the
Davidic line would narrow the field of would-be rulers;
while the stress on the devastating effects of idolatry would
serve as a warning to the infant nation.

Ezra

It is generally conceded that Ezra was the author of
the book which bears his name. He was born in Babylon
and there "prepared his heart to seek the law of the Lord,
and to do it, and to teach in Israel statutes and judgments" (Ezra 7:10). His birth as a descendant of Aaron
qualified him to be a priest and allowed him access to
the books of the law. He became a scribe, an office of
importance in ancient times. His skill in writing, coupled
with his access to documents, and his authority as a priest
support the view that he was the compiler-editor of
Samuel, Kings, and Chronicles.

The books of Ezra and Nehemiah are a record of the fulfillment of prophecy, though there is no mention of this in the texts themselves. Isaiah had prophesied that Judah would return. He even went so far as to name the emperor (Cyrus) who would allow them to rebuild the temple (Isaiah 44:28). Jeremiah also had prophesied of Judah's delivery, stating that the captivity would last seventy years (Jeremiah 25:12; 29:10). Ezra recounted the decree issued by the Persian emperor, Cyrus, which let a contingent of Jews return to Jerusalem to begin the work. Under the direction of Zerubbabel, the governor of this first group, the proper forms of worship were reestablished and the rebuilding of the temple was begun. Ezra recorded the opposition to the work by the Samaritans, descendants of Babylonians and others who had intermarried with Israelites who had not been carried away by the Assyrians. (The religion of these Samaritans mixed some adapted teachings of Judaism with pagan practices.) The Jews were able to overcome the opposition for a while and the work continued.

Ezra told how the Persian emperor, Artaxerxes, commissioned him to bring another contingent of exiles to Judah. He solicited priests, Levites, and others necessary to staff the temple. Thus, by the time the temple was rebuilt, the personnel were on hand to begin its operation. The book ends with an account of a reform movement, pushed by Ezra, to rid Judah of the evil influences caused by the intermarriage of the Jews with local pagan women who refused to worship Jehovah.

One purpose of the book of Ezra may be to expose the mercy of God as he works through the historical process. Its main message is to record how the returning exiles attempted to reestablish true worship and to guard against the repetition of the sins which had led their fathers into captivity.

Nehemiah

The book of Nehemiah is a companion to the book of Ezra. Indeed, the two authors were contemporaries. Nehemiah brought a third contingent of Jews from Babylon about thirteen years after Ezra's contingent. There is some disagreement on the chronology presented in these two books, as the apocryphal books of Ezdras and the works of Josephus suggest a different sequence. Some authorities feel that Nehemiah arrived first. (D. Guthrie and J. A. Motyer, eds., *The New Bible Commentary*, rev. ed. [Grand Rapids, Mi.: Wm. B. Eerdmans Publishing Co., 1970], pages 395-96.) Unfortunately, there is not enough knowledge available at present to decide the issue. The historicity of the component parts of these two books is not in question, however, only their order. Whatever the case, it is certain that Ezra and Nehemiah worked together to secure Jerusalem and reestablish the Jews on a solid basis in the land.

The book of Nehemiah tells how he had risen in Babylon to the high and trusted position of cupbearer to Artaxerxes. This position allowed him to keep track of the affairs in Jerusalem. Hearing of the poor conditions of the Jews there, he prayed that God would prepare a way for him to help. Shortly thereafter the opportunity arose for him to present the case of his people to the emperor, who responded by giving Nehemiah authority and funds to rebuild the walls of Jerusalem. After his arrival in Jerusalem, he went to work on this project. The thought of a strong Jerusalem created consternation among non-Jewish rulers in the area, however, and they tried to stop the work. Nehemiah armed his builders and was successful in completing the walls and setting up the gates. Reforms were instituted through which poor and indebted Jews were forgiven of their debts and given land. Priests without genealogical records were denied the priesthood. Intermarriage with non-Jews was discouraged.

During this time Ezra finished his work of restoring the scriptures. The law of Moses was read and interpreted in public gatherings. This was because the vast majority had ceased to speak Hebrew and had substituted the language of the peoples among whom they lived in Babylon. This language was Aramaic. It was necessary for the scribes to read and translate for the people. After hearing the law, the Jews covenanted not to depart from it again.

Nehemiah returned to the Persian courts after a time but after a stay of unknown duration was able to get leave to return again to Jerusalem. Upon his return he instituted further reforms including Sabbath observance, reverence for the priesthood, and the exclusion of Ammonites and Moabites from the congregation of the Jews. It was during this time that the Jews became extremely aware of the law. Some joined into sects composed of fanatics who insisted on total observance of the whole law and then went beyond, making up additional rules of their own to assure compliance. These eventually became known as the Pharisees.

Esther

The events recorded in this book took place about the same time as those recorded in Nehemiah. Thus, Esther is a companion to the books of Ezra and Nehemiah. The author of the work is unknown, as is the book's manner of transmission into the sacred literature. There is no doubt it belongs there, however, for again one is shown the hand of God working behind the scenes to fulfill his covenant.

Esther chronicles the ascent of the orphaned Jewess, Hadassah, later known as Queen Esther, to the station of Queen of the Persian Empire and wife of Artaxerxes, who was called Ahasuerus in the Bible. Her husband was persuaded through the lies of his prime minister, Haman, to issue an edict of extermination against all Jews. At considerable risk to her own life, Esther was able to reveal the plot to the king before the edict was executed, thus saving herself and all the Jews.

It is of interest that the author did not ascribe Esther's success directly to God. It was intimated, however, when Mordecai, Esther's cousin and stepfather, encouraged her to take the steps necessary to stop Haman and said, "Who knoweth whether thou art come to the kingdom for such a time as this?" Thus he implied that neither her birth nor her ascent to queenly station were mere chance. But detailing the work of God does not seem to be the purpose of the author. Rather, he seemed to assume that the reader would understand that. So he focused on what some commentators have assumed was his own objective: to explain the origin of the celebration of the holiday known as "Purim" (celebrated as a remembrance of the salvation arranged by Esther) and to record the high stations achieved by Esther and Mordecai.

POETRY AND WISDOM LITERATURE

Poetry, especially in the form of a song or hymn,

played an important part in the lives of the ancient Israelites. Therefore, it is not surprising to find a section of their
sacred literature devoted to it. Not all biblical poetry is
found in this section, however. Many of the prophets were
poets, and there are major passages in their works which
are poetic, as well as a number of kinds of poetic composition. Among these were *sir*, a song with or without
instrumental accompaniment; *mizmor*, a psalm or hymn
with musical accompaniment; *qina*, an elegy or lament;
tehilla, a hymn of praise; and *masal*, both a proverb and a
satirical song. As can be seen, many of the poems were
set to music. The Jews were evidently a music-loving
people and famous throughout the ancient world for their
songs. (J. D. Douglas, ed., *The New Bible Dictionary*, s.v.
"Psalms, book of" [Grand Rapids, Mi.: Wm. B. Eerdmans Publishing Co., 1962].) The greatest collection of
these today is in the book of Psalms.

Associated with the poetry was the "wisdom literature." This genre of literature was common to the ancient
Near East. It consisted of instructions for successful living or
an analysis of the perplexities of the human condition.
There were two main types: proverbial wisdom consisting
of short, pithy sayings which set rules by which happiness
and benefit would come (for example, Proverbs) and specu-
lative wisdom using monologues (for example, Ecclesiastes),
or dialogues (for example, Job) to delve into such problems
as the meaning of existence and man's relationship with
God. The Hebrews adopted the practice of collecting the
wisdom material and applying it to their lives. For them
true wisdom stemmed from God. Therefore, the prophets
provided the channel through which it flowed. Real wisdom consisted of the application of prophetic truth to one's
life.

Job

Greater controversy has arisen over the book of Job in relation to its principal personality and authorship than any other book in the Bible. Many believe the book to be an allegory about humanity in general and, therefore, not to be taken as history. For them, Job is a fictional character. Others insist that Job was a real person whose suffering in mortality was known and used by a later writer as the subject of his work. Still others insist that Job was a real person who wrote his own material. Even these disagree when he lived. Some place him as early as Abraham, others after the Babylonian captivity. At present, the controversy cannot be resolved. Even latter-day scripture is of little help. From the one reference to him found therein (D&C 121:10) it could be argued that he was a historical figure, but that is all.

The one aspect of this book about which there is agreement is its high literary quality. As a poem it stands unexcelled by even the majesty of the works of Isaiah. The work is a "theodicy" in that it investigates and tries to solve the problem of why the righteous suffer injustice and evil. The investigation takes the form of a discussion between Job, three friends, and a young man. These go through three cycles. In each, all three of Job's friends offer their views on why Job is suffering. After each has expressed his view, Job offers a rebuttal. Finally, a young man enters and offers his opinion, after which Jehovah speaks and appears to Job and vindicates him.

It is generally believed that the question raised by Job is never answered. After completing the book one is still unsure of why the righteous suffer. But in this case the restored gospel supplies answers the world does not have.

Seeing Job as a perfect man, the world cannot understand why God would deal with him as described in the story. The message of the book centers in the fact that Job's perfection was relative to his station. But God's designs, knowing the power within the man, were to push him to an even higher level of perfection. Therefore, he placed him in a position where he had to be more patient, more kind, more long-suffering, more trusting than he ever had been before. And what was the result of Job's endurance? He was pushed to the level of perfection that allowed him to come into the presence of God. In this light the book vindicates God and shows that all things work for the good of those who love Him. One of the great insights in this book is found in chapters 29 to 31, where Job presents his case to the Lord and describes the conduct of a perfect man. It is clear that the physical care of those in need, and chastity that includes a pure mind, are the main characteristics that epitomize a perfect man.

Psalms

The Hebrew title of this work would translate "song of praise." Since over half of the psalms were written in praise of Jehovah, the title is appropriate for the whole collection. The title in the English Bible comes from the Septuagint, where it is called "the Psaltery," which also is the name of a musical instrument with strings. The psalms were a kind of hymn sung to the accompaniment of a psalter. The Hebrews called the individual psalms *mizmor* from the Hebrew word *zamar* meaning "to cut off." Probably this term was adopted because each word in the psalm was separated into syllables and a note was supplied for each syllable. (Clarke, 3:199.)

David is given credit for most of the psalms, and there is no doubt that he composed about half of them. The rest were written by various men, some of whom were contemporaries of David. In the King James Version of the Bible we find the following breakdown according to author and number written: David, seventy-three; Solomon, two; the sons of Korah, ten; Asaph, twelve; Heman, one; Ethan, one; psalms bearing no name, fifty-nine. Ezra is credited with having gathered, edited, and arranged the order of the psalms, thus providing Judah with a standard hymnal as part of their sacred literature.

Of all the books of the Old Testament this one most seems to breathe the essence of Christianity. Attesting to this is the fact that, of the 283 direct quotes from the Old Testament cited in the New Testament, 116 were taken from Psalms. Such love of the psalms by the early Christians came because of the insights into the nature, goodness, mercy, and mission of the Lord which are revealed in many of these inspired poems.

Proverbs

The term *proverb* comes from the Latin *pro* meaning "for" and *verbum* meaning "a word, speech, or saying." Thus a proverb is a short saying which stands for a whole discourse. The Hebrews call the collection *meshalim*, from *mashal*, which signifies that which is weighty, wise, and therefore authoritative.

The book is generally attributed to Solomon. Supposedly he collected wise sayings from those who preceded him as well as setting forth many himself. This notion is borne out by the structure of the book itself. The first part (chapters 1-8) represents the admonitions, directions, and cautions of a teacher to a student. The second part (chapters 9-22:16) contains the proverbs of Solomon proper. The third part (chapters 22:17—25:28) again contains instructions of a teacher to a student. The fourth part (chapters 26-29) is stated to be a collection of Solomon's proverbs made by men (probably Isaiah, Hosea, and Micah) under the direction of King Hezekiah. The final portion (chapters 30-31) forms a kind of appendix in which the teacher, Agur, instructs his pupils, Ithiel and Ucal, and an unnamed mother instructs her son Lemuel. The final form of the book is accredited by many scholars to Ezra.

The purpose of Proverbs is stated in the first chapter: "The fear [i.e. awe, reverence, and love] of the Lord is the beginning of knowledge" (Proverbs 1:7). Though there is much in the book which does not rise above worldly wisdom, the whole serves as a reminder that all things are spiritual. Further, it serves to underscore the idea that even in mortal life, when properly viewed, all things testify of God.

Ecclesiastes

The name of this book is a transliteration of a Greek translation of the Hebrew word *koheleth*, which signifies one who calls a meeting. From this comes the reference to the work as "the preacher." The *koheleth* refers to himself in Ecclesiastes 1:1 as the "son of David, king in Jerusalem," and from this many have concluded that this is another work of Solomon. This title could refer to any royal descendant of David, however. Also, the linguistic evidence does not support Solomon's authorship, since the Hebrew is reflective of a later stage of development that seems to date the book after his time. Still, the work has the flavor and force of inspired writing and has been unquestioned by Jew or Christian on that ground. It is powerfully written in sparkling prose that is set down in meter.

Ecclesiastes is a brilliant essay on the ultimate pursuit of life—that which is best to do. Ultimately the writer demonstrates the fact that every pursuit is vain except fearing God and keeping his commandments. This, he says, "is the whole duty of man"; because everything is to be brought "into judgment" (Ecclesiastes 12:13-14). Of course, all other pursuits *do* take on meaning when one's focus is on obedience to God. Thus, the author encourages his reader to do all things with his might, because this mortal life only comes once and is the basis of the judgment and all that follows it (Ecclesiastes 9:10). The book has far more meaning to someone who has the perspective of the plan of salvation. Others have grossly misunderstood it and have misused passages in it to support the idea that there is no life between death and the resurrection and other perversions of Old Testament Christianity.

Song of Solomon

This book in the Hebrew is called "Song of Songs," a phrase which denotes a song selected above others because of its excellence. Actually, it is not a song but an ode containing many beautiful phrases and much lyrical prose. Though its authorship is ascribed to Solomon, its linguistic style is exactly the same as Ecclesiastes, pointing to a late date of composition. The right of this book to be a part of sacred literature has been questioned by both Jews and Christians. It has retained its place on the argument that it is an allegory setting forth the love of God for Israel or of Christ for his church. In the manuscript of the Joseph Smith Translation is a note stating that the work is not inspired scripture. (Robert J. Matthews, *A Plainer Translation: Joseph Smith's Translation of the Bible* [Provo, Ut.: Brigham Young University Press, 1975], pages 87, 215.)

THE PROPHETS

Though many prophets are referred to in the Old Testament, the works of only sixteen have been preserved as separate books. These prophets labored at various periods of Israelite history. Though not all of their ministries can be dated precisely, the following order might prove helpful in establishing their relationship to Israel's history and to one another.

1. Jonah, probably at the time of Jeroboam II (ca. 795 B.C.)
2. Hosea, at the time of Uzziah, Jotham, and Ahaz (ca. 790 B.C.)
3. Joel, at the time of Hosea (ca. 790 B.C.)
4. Amos, at the time of Uzziah (ca. 782 B.C.)
5. Isaiah, begins ministry at time of Jotham (ca. 740 B.C.)
6. Micah, at the time of Isaiah (ca. 722 B.C.)
7. Nahum, probably at the time of Amon and Josiah (ca. 642 B.C.)
8. Zephaniah, at the time of Josiah (ca. 640 B.C.)
9. Jeremiah, from Josiah to Zedekiah (ca. 628 B.C.)
10. Obadiah, probably at the time of Jehoahaz (ca. 609 B.C.)
11. Daniel, carried into Babylon (ca. 606 B.C.)
12. Habakkuk, at time of Zedekiah (ca. 598 B.C.)
13. Ezekiel, during the captivity (ca. 598 B.C.)
14. Haggai, at time of Darius II (ca. 424 B.C.)
15. Zechariah, at about same time as Haggai (ca. 420 B.C.)
16. Malachi, at time of Ezra and Nehemiah (ca. 430 B.C.)

The Major Prophets

The above prophets are divided into two groups called the major, former, or greater prophets, and the minor, latter, or lesser prophets. This in no way reflects on their ministries nor their prophecies but on the length of the books that carry their names and the position in which they are placed in the Old Testament. In this section the works of the major prophets will be reviewed.

Isaiah. Isaiah was a prophet to all the house of Israel. The time of his ministry saw the formation of those world powers which would lead to empire building on scales never known before. The foundations of spiritual Babylon had been laid centuries earlier in the days of Nimrod. Many kingdoms would rise and fall, but the undergirding structure common to them all would remain. It was against this that spiritual Israel in all dispensations would have to compete. Standing as he did at a moment when these forces of Babylon were very active both in and out of Israel, and wrapped in the vision of a seer, which allowed him to see the history of Israel to the end of time, Isaiah became a type of universal prophet whose message is to all Israel through all dispensations.

Much debate has gone on as to whether all the material in this book can be ascribed to Isaiah or if the work is a composite of a number of writers working over the course of a few hundred years. The reason for this debate is that some of the specifics about which Isaiah prophesied occurred long after his death. Those without faith insist that such are additions to the record written after the fact. But no manuscript of the book yet found, no matter how ancient, suggests anything but the authorship of one man. For the Latter-day Saint, there is additional evidence. Much of Isaiah was copied into the Book of Mormon record. That which is there establishes Isaiah as the sole author of the book which bears his name.

Isaiah's ministry centered in Jerusalem and covered a span of about forty years — generally considered to be from 740 B.C. to 701 B.C. Except that he was the son of Amoz, nothing concrete is known of his ancestry. Traditions indicate that he was of royal descent and a cousin to the king whom he served. That he had a family is known from his record. His wife was a prophetess who bore him at least two children. He died, again according to tradition, as a martyr, being "sawn asunder" during the reign of Manasseh.

Of all the Old Testament prophets, none is quoted more frequently in all the standard works than is Isaiah. This is because his message is so universal and of such high poetic quality. His words are at times difficult to understand, however. This arises from his frequent use of symbolism, his poetic style, and his prophetic insight. The latter allowed him to view not only his own time but all time in a kind of cosmic setting. Therefore, themes coming out of his time are not only applicable to his day but to later times as well. Consequently, some of his prophecies have more than one application or are fulfilled more than once. The best helps in understanding him are the Book of Mormon and the Doctrine and Covenants. The extensive use of Isaiah in these books places many of his words into a concrete setting or precise meaning, allowing a greater understanding of the rest. (For a helpful LDS commentary on the book of Isaiah which incorporates comments by General Authorities of the Church, see Monte S. Nyman, *Great Are the Words of Isaiah* [Salt Lake City: Bookcraft, 1980].)

The writings of Isaiah carry messages of warning to apostate Israel and prophecies of the scattering and gather-

ing of Israel. But even more impressive are his prophecies
about the Savior. It is Jesus that gives meaning to all of
Isaiah. Therefore, the more one reads Isaiah the better he
understands the nature and mission of the Savior and the
relationship of that mission to the covenant with Israel
which allows those of us living in the latter days to have the
gospel of Jesus Christ, partake of priesthood power, gather
Israel, and be prepared to meet the Lord.

Jeremiah. There is more knowledge about the life of
Jeremiah than any other prophet in the Old Testament.
He was born, of priestly descent, at Anathoth, a small
village about four miles northeast of Jerusalem, about 645
B.C. He was called to the ministry when he was in his late
teens, and he continued his ministry for over forty years. He
witnessed the events from the dissolution of the Assyrian
Empire to the fall of the kingdom of Judah at the hands of
the Babylonians in 587 B.C. In all of this he was not a dis-
passionate observer but rather an ardent patriot. Throughout his long ministry he worked to persuade Judah to turn
from her evil, which would destroy their country, and
follow the Lord. For this he suffered rejection, plots against
his life, mobbings, imprisonment, and, if certain traditions
are correct, martyrdom in Egypt. (There are contradictory
traditions.)

The book of Jeremiah appears to be a compilation of
writings and prophecies that are not necessarily chrono-
logical. Also, there are sketches of his life and ministry
arranged, perhaps, after his death, but nonetheless his own
work. Though not of the elegance of Isaiah, Jeremiah's
writing is still sublime and powerful. Through it one sees the
burden of grief the prophet carried as the people refused to
heed his warnings. Knowing by the spirit of prophecy what

the end result would be, he was doubly burdened. Not only would the people be deprived of the spirit and blessings of God, but they would suffer excruciating misery until only a small remnant would remain alive.

The people of his day insisted fanatically that as long as they observed the rites of the temple God would not let them fall. This gave rise to the major message of the book. External service to God is not what counts if there is an absence of righteousness and purity within the heart. Outward performances and reform are empty and useless unless there is an inward regeneration which develops fellowship with God. It is the heart which makes all performances and ordinances efficacious and brings the blessings of heaven.

Lamentations.   This book was written shortly after the destruction of Jerusalem and the fall of the Southern Kingdom. It fully exposed the pathos felt by Jeremiah as he watched and was a part of that tragedy. Though forcefully depicted by David in a few psalms, nowhere can one find a more successful picture of bodily misery and mental agony. With every word one can almost hear the drop of a tear and feel the breaking of a heart.

The book is a series of acrostic (featuring alphabetic succession) poems. Chapters 1, 2, and 4 each have twenty-two verses beginning with words that start with successive letters of the Hebrew alphabet. Chapter 3 has sixty-six verses, every third one beginning in a similar fashion. Chapter 5 is not alphabetical (acrostic).

The book is instructive not only because of the picture it paints of the scenes of destruction and the feelings of the people, but because it stresses that Judah brought the suffering on herself. Whereas the suffering of an individual or a gentile nation cannot necessarily be attributed to sin, the suffering of a covenant nation can be. The Jews had reached a level of desperate wickedness which God could not ignore. His own house had been thoroughly polluted. But in all this darkness there was a spark of light. Though God is justice and judgment, he also is mercy. If Israel would repent and call upon the Lord, Jeremiah promised that the Lord would hear and a restoration would be possible.

Ezekiel. From what can be gathered, Ezekiel did not receive his prophetic call until after his deportation to Babylon. He was the son of Buzi and was also a priest. He settled with other exiles in a village on the Chebar River. There his ministry began, and it continued for about twenty-two years. His message to his people was not initially one of consolation but of continued reproof. The Jews, in spite of all their punishments, continued their rebellion and idolatry. As the exile continued over the next seventy years, a degree of piety did develop. That Ezekiel saw the beginning of such fruit of his work is possible. The shift in emphasis which his writings reveal suggests that he did.

Ezekiel, like other Old Testament prophets, was an extraordinary poet, which accounts for much of the interweaving of symbolism and imagery in his message. The use of this method probably gave force to his words. He captured and held the attention of his people. Unfortunately, his style sometimes hampers the modern reader. The major portion of his prophecy, however, is intelligible and edifying to today's reader.

Ezekiel can be broken into three divisions. The first portion (chapters 1-24) recounts the judgments against Jerusalem and Judah. The middle portion (chapters 25-39) deals with the eventual restoration not only of Judah but all the house of Israel. The final section (chapters 40-48) deals with the building of the latter-day temple and the nature of worship there.

The message of the work is varied. Of particular interest are his vision of the valley of dry bones, the uniting of the sticks (records) of Ephraim and Judah, a description of the battle of Armageddon, and a picture of the millennial reign of the Lord. Undergirding all this, as with other prophets, is the testimony that the work of the kingdom is God's. God's purposes are not frustrated but will all be fulfilled. The best course of action for the individual, therefore, is to follow the Lord.

Daniel. Like Ezekiel, Daniel was a victim of the fall of the kingdom of Judah. They were taken captive to Babylon — Daniel in 602 B.C. and Ezekiel somewhat later. In the 602 B.C. episode, the Babylonians took hostages from Jerusalem to their capital in an effort to assure Jewish loyalty to their cause. Many of the hostages were children of nobles. For this reason it is presumed that Daniel was of royal birth, though nothing is known of his ancestry. In Babylon, he and three companions were educated in the royal courts. He was able to distinguish himself, not only for his understanding and wisdom but for his strong piety as well. Through his gift of interpreting dreams, he eventually became governor of the province of Babylon. His wisdom became proverbial (as intimated in Ezekiel 14:14, 20) even in his own day. Such high station resulted in jealousy and a plot to kill him. This was foiled by divine intervention.

The book of Daniel is unique to the Old Testament because of its apocalyptic nature. Where other prophets dwelt somewhat on the future, the burden of their messages predicted imminent disaster. Daniel, on the other hand, looked to the far future and dwelt on the joyous theme of the establishment of the kingdom of God and the coming of the Son of God in the last days.

As a writer Daniel cannot be ranked with the poets. His work is straight prose, written partly in Hebrew and partly in Chaldean. Daniel was a master in both languages. His work divides easily into two sections: the first (chapters 1-6) deals with his personal history; the second (chapters 7-12) with his prophetic visions.

The message of the book of Daniel is one of happiness and hope. This historical portion emphasizes the blessings that come to those who maintain their integrity and righteousness under all circumstances. The prophetic portion emphasizes the eventual and ultimate triumph of good over all the forces of evil.

The Minor Prophets

Hosea. The ministry of Hosea appears to have been a long one. If the information in the superscription (Hosea 1:1) is correct, he could have labored from about 809 B.C. to 698 B.C.—over 110 years. Many have doubted this to be accurate and have placed his death about 736 B.C., since his book contains no allusion to the Syro-Ephraimitic war which occurred about that time, nor of the deportation of the Northern Kingdom under Tiglath-Pileser a few years later. Even so, his ministry still stretched over forty-five years, making it one of the longest among the prophets. Nothing is known of his ancestry except that he was the son of Beeri. (Clarke, 4:620.) Jewish tradition states that Beeri was a prince in the tribe of Reuben. Hosea's field of labor was the Northern Kingdom, in which he was born, and he is the only prophet whose labors were confined to that area by whom there are written prophecies.

Hosea's married life was tragic. His wife, Gomer, was either an idolator or a harlot. Her life with Hosea is used by the Lord as an allegory to describe the faithlessness of Israel. Like Jehovah, Hosea did all he could to reform his erring wife. Israel rejected the covenant on the false belief that the pagan nations around her were the source of her sustenance and power. So the Lord cast out Israel like an unfaithful wife to suffer the consequences of her actions— with the hope that she would learn her folly. Because of the love of God, this rejection would not be a permanent condition. If Israel would repent, forgiveness and acceptance would be granted. Thus, though full of prophecies of doom, the book of Hosea is one of love and hope. Continually the prophet looked to the last days when Israel would receive the Lord. In this way he showed that God's love will never fail. But there was more. As love is the source of her redemption so, too, it is the foundation of her punishment. God will allow her vexation as the means by which Israel might be purified and brought to repentance.

Joel. It is difficult, if not impossible, to assign a definite date to the ministry of Joel. It could have been as early as 850 B.C. or as late as 450 B.C. Only two things are known for sure: he was the son of Pethuel, and he ministered to the kingdom of Judah. Except for the introduction (Joel 1:1) his name is mentioned neither in his own book nor in the rest of the Bible. Nonetheless, his writings are of such import, especially for those living in the last days, that Moroni quoted part of his prophecies to Joseph Smith (see Joseph Smith—History:41).

If the date of his ministry is unknown, the setting of his prophecy is clear. Judah was threatened by a severe plague of locusts coupled with drought. Terrible famine would be

the result. Judah was promised this would be averted on the
condition of repentance.

It is possible that Joel was using the locusts, in their
various destructive stages, symbolically and that the reality
was invasion and captivity by foreign powers. Whatever
the case, this prophecy acted as the springboard into his
other prophecies. These also dealt with an invasion, but this
time it definitely was one of vast armies and was set in the
last days. Unlike the former invasion, the latter will result in
victory for repentant and gathered Israel. Indeed, according
to his writings, the days at the time of the coming of the
Son of God will be filled with revelation, vision and power
for the people of God.

Amos. Being from Tekoa, a little town twelve miles
south of Jerusalem, Amos was a Judean prophet sent to
prophesy against Israel. He ministered around 750 B.C. He
was called from his work as a herdsman and a gatherer of
sycamore fruit. Such work indicates that he came from the
lowest levels of society. His literary ability seems to belie this
idea, however. Some Jewish scholars have surmised that he
was a temple functionary in charge of the flocks used in
temple worship. (*Encyclopedia Judaica*, s.v. ''Amos.'') All this
is conjecture, as is the idea that he was born in Tekoa.
The fact that he gathered sycamore fruit, which grows in the
low hills, not in the higher Judean mountains, would suggest a more northern homeland. If this is the case, then he
was probably from Israel but was forced to flee into Judea
after his confrontation with the idolatrous high priest,
Amaziah, at Bethel. This forced banishment did not stop
him from prophesying.

Amos's ministry began two years before an earth-
quake of note. His initial work consisted of that recorded in

chapters one and seven. His first message was a wholesale condemnation of all the nations surrounding the Dead Sea and the Sea of Galilee, Israel and Judah being threatened the most. Indeed, their punishment would be the greater because they had rejected the greater light. This punishment would stop short of total destruction and in the last days the kingdom would not only be restored but would surpass its ancient glory.

The emphasis of Amos's writing centers on the moral character of God, the righteous ruler of all nations. All are subject unto him, especially Israel and Judah. They must heed the prophets whom God will always send to warn mankind or they must suffer the consequences. Amos further shows that, with God, it is the intent of the heart that counts. The act of sacrifice, if not done in righteousness, avails nothing.

Obadiah. This is the shortest book in the Old Testament. Nothing is definitely known about Obadiah. If he is the Obadiah mentioned in 1 Kings 18:3, then he was the chief steward of King Ahab who saved the prophets of God from the wrath of Jezebel. The context of his prophecy makes this timing doubtful, however, since the setting is directly after some capture of Jerusalem. This is more likely the capture by the Babylonians in 586 B.C.

The prophecy of Obadiah is against Edom. It condemns Edom not only because Edom refused to help its brother Israel, but because it actually helped the enemy. For this reason God would allow it to be destroyed. The message of Obadiah works in concert with that of Amos, underscoring the idea that God is indeed the God of all nations. All nations are, therefore, subject to his law to some degree. But this is not all. Nations, especially those related by blood, have a moral obligation to one another which must be honored, or punishment will follow.

Jonah. It is likely that this prophet ministered during the reign of Jeroboam II about 800 B.C. This is based on the fact that a prophet by this name was laboring at that time (2 Kings 14-25). The book itself only tells us the prophet was from Gath-hepher, a small town in northern Israel. It gives no hint as to the time of his ministry, though it must have taken place before the destruction of Nineveh in 606 B.C., since Jonah's mission was to preach there.

It is most probable that this book, unlike the other books of the minor prophets listed so far, was not written by the person whose name it bears but about him. This is not to say that Jonah was not a historical figure, but that he did not author the material we now have; that a later author used this well-known story to make a point to people living long after Jonah's day. This probably accounts for the fact that this book is different (containing only one verse of prophecy, the rest being history) than any of the others belonging to the minor prophets.

Jonah was written in beautiful Hebrew poetry. It has one central message—that God is the God of all nations and also the God of love—which encompasses those of Amos, Obadiah, and Hosea. Therefore, he will warn and forgive others besides Israel. The Lord sent Jonah to warn Nineveh. Like many bearers of the priesthood, Jonah was reluctant to fulfill his calling; but the Lord insisted that he complete his mission. Nineveh repented and was saved, emphasizing the point that God is, indeed, a God of mercy and a God of love.

Micah. This prophet was from the town of Moresheth-gath on the southern plains of Judah. His ministry seems to have covered a span of over forty years, during part of which Hezekiah was king of Judah. Nothing is known of his personal life. During his time the Northern Kingdom was destroyed.

His work can be divided into three parts. In the first part he rebuked both Samaria and Jerusalem for their gross iniquities and predicted that both would fall. This led into the next section where he showed that both would eventually return and become glorious. The final section mixed both warning and hope.

It is interesting that Micah did not restrict his message to one kingdom or the other. His prophecies, both of condemnation and restoration, were for both. This is not surprising, since Micah acknowledged only one king over both kingdoms—Jehovah. Therefore, what pertained to one pertained to the other. There was no double standard. The hope of both, he taught, was based on the advent of the divine ruler who would come out of Bethlehem of Judea. In the day when this king would reign all the House of Israel would be glorious. Here his message joined that of Hosea. Again, God was shown to be filled with love and mercy. Because of this all Israel would be redeemed at the last day.

Nahum. Tradition identifies this prophet as a resident of Galilee, stating that the little town of Elkosh from which he came was in that area. Nothing is known of the man himself. He ministered between the fall of No-Amon (Thebes) in Egypt about 660 B.C. and that of Nineveh in 606 B.C. Though the work was written as though the events it described had already happened, the fact that it is a vision suggests that it is prophetic and therefore was written some years before 606 B.C.

The whole work is one unit. It is a poem of exultation describing the downfall of hated Nineveh. This act is depicted as the vengeance of a just God on the oppressors of his people. Nahum overlooked the sins of Israel as he focused on the fall of her oppressors. In doing so, he indirectly revealed that, so far as God is concerned, one nation has no right to subdue another, no matter how wicked the victim is. Such an act will not go unpunished, because the Lord is the Sovereign of all the world, and it is his responsibility to punish the unrighteous. He is the avenger or champion of his people and the source of security for those who trust him.

Habakkuk.   Nothing is known of the life or ministry of this prophet. Internal evidence in the poem itself suggests that he lived during the ascendency of Babylon about the time the Assyrian nation fell. This would put his prophecies about 600 B.C.

The book of Habakkuk has much in common with the book of Job. Both deal with the question of why the righteous suffer. Both come to the same answer but in different ways. Habakkuk complains that God allows violence and injustice to prevail against the righteous. The divine answer that wickedness will not go unavenged, for the Chaldeans (Babylonians) will be the means of punishing Israel's former oppressors, does not satisfy him. The deliverance was to a new enemy who would continue the injustices. God assures the prophet that all wickedness will eventually be overcome. In the meantime, God will use it to further his own purposes. During that time the righteous must live by faith. Exercising such faith during his own life, Habakkuk, like Job before him, is prepared through trial to view the Savior. On the basis of the understanding which comes from this experience, he closes his book with the firm assurance that no matter what the present might bring, his trust will be in the Lord.

Zephaniah. If the Hezekiah mentioned in the introduction of this book as the great-grandfather of Zephaniah was the former king of Judah, then Zephaniah was a relative of Josiah during whose reign he served. His ministry seems to have broken a fifty-year period of prophetic silence, and it gives emphasis to the reforms attempted by Josiah to win the people back to Jehovah. Nothing is known of the personal life of Zephaniah.

Zephaniah first prophesied of universal judgment, in this section giving not one word of hope. All was doom and darkness. Judah and all her neighbors were to fall in the great day of the Lord. One almost wonders if any would be spared. Then Zephaniah turned to the future. In exultation he saw the people humbled, restored, and purified, worshipping at the mountain of the Lord's house. The prophet then broke into a joyous hymn of Zion in which Jehovah was shown to have taken away the sentence on the house of Israel and to have given it victory. His use of the Zion theme dramatized his belief that the future was totally in Jehovah's hands. Only he can bring about the Restoration and bequeath the spirit of humility and righteousness by which salvation can come.

Haggai. This prophet's ministry began after the return of the Jews from Babylon. He apparently began his ministry before the arrival of Nehemiah, for his first recorded words were addressed to the first governor of Jerusalem, Zerubbabel. Though nothing is known of his personal life, it is fairly certain that he was born in Babylon and that he returned to Jerusalem with some of the first party. From the context of his book, it would appear that he was well known and respected before the incidents and prophecies in his book were given.

Haggai was upset over the slowness of the people to begin work on the house of the Lord. He told them that the poverty, famine, and drought they were experiencing was a direct result of their procrastination. His preaching had the desired effect and work got under way. The poverty of many of the people made it impossible to adorn the house with the richness it had before. Haggai encouraged those of his people sensitive to this by stating that the day of the Lord was near, at which time the house would have more glory than ever before. He warned them though that, just as the touch of the unclean pollutes all around it, so does a people remain unclean without the cleaning touch of the temple. Only when the temple was built would God's loving-kindness fully return. In support of this, and as a sign of God's acceptance for the work already done, he declared that from that moment on they would be blessed with good harvest.

Haggai desired to have the people look with hope to the future. Their present distress would pass if they would labor. In this way they would achieve the great things the Lord had in store for them.

Zechariah.   Haggai was not alone in his ministry. About two months after his work began he was joined by Zechariah, son of Berechiah, son of Iddo, who also was a prophet. The book of Nehemiah tells of a priest named Zechariah of the family of Iddo, who is very possibly this prophet. As with other prophets, very little is known of his personal life.

His writings, which are full of visions and prophecy, are the longest and the most difficult of all the minor prophets. His visions are highly symbolic, and he drifts back and forth in time from his day to the time of the Lord's first and second comings. His messianic prophecies are some of the most pointed and clear in all the scriptures, however. He speaks of the Messiah as being lowly, riding upon a colt, the foal of an ass; of his betrayal for thirty pieces of silver; and of the battle of Armageddon, at which time all of Judah will be converted to the Lord.

Zechariah attributed the destruction of Solomon's Temple and the exile to sin, and connected redemption with repentance. He foretold the destruction of Babylon by Darius I about two years before it took place, warning the large Jewish population of that city of the impending doom. It is most likely that they took advantage of this to remove themselves from the city to their homeland or some other place of security. (Clarke, 4:766.)

It is this fall of ancient Babylon which supplied the uniting thread through the varied tapestry of Zechariah. Babylon became the scriptural symbol of Satan's counterfeit of Zion, or the wicked world. And Babylon's downfall became symbolic of the future downfall of Satan's kingdom. This took on even greater meaning as Zechariah saw in vision the work and eventual fall of spiritual Babylon. He saw that the "Branch" would ultimately destroy Babylon. Jesus is the "Branch," of course—see Isaiah 11:1. Many keys to the prophecies of Zechariah are found in a revelation to Joseph Smith. (See D&C 45:11-60; also the Inspired Version, Matthew 24; also Joseph Smith—History.)

Malachi. The ministry of Malachi marks the close of the prophetic voice in Judah until the fervent cry of John the Baptist about four hundred years later. (Of course, there may have been other prophets whose records are lost.) So little is known about this prophet that scholars have credited his work to others, such as Ezra. Through modern revelation, however, it is known that he was a real person with great prophetic power. (See D&C 138:46.) Apparently his ministry closed around 430 B.C.

The book of Malachi is small, but every word is great with meaning to all future generations. The Savior dictated the last two chapters to the Nephites so that they and we might have them. (See 3 Nephi 25, 26:1, 2.) Further, in our own time, the angel Moroni quoted portions of Malachi to Joseph Smith.

Malachi first castigated the priests for neglecting and abusing their sacred office. Then he rebuked the people for failing to pay their tithes and offerings. He also scolded them for divorces and for marriages to foreign women. But perhaps the most important message of Malachi was his prophecy of Elijah's return. Elijah was translated so that he might restore the sealing keys. By these, and only by these, is it possible for men and women to marry for eternity and thereby perpetuate the family in eternity. In Malachi's day the people were not only disrespectful of their marriage vows but were going so far as to marry outside the covenant. Malachi warned that such persons would be left with neither root nor branch (i.e., ancestry and posterity). Malachi looked to another day when the priesthood would respect its office, having been purged by the Lord so that the hearts of the people would be turned to their ancestors and posterity. Then would the sealing power of Elijah be upon them.

CONCLUSION

As mentioned in the forepart of this chapter, the word of God is most precious. The Old Testament contains much of that word. In it is verified the modern statement of the

Lord: "For God doth not walk in crooked paths, neither doth he turn to the right hand nor to the left, neither doth he vary from that which he hath said, therefore his paths are straight, and his course is one eternal round." (D&C 3:2.)

God is a God of justice and judgment, but he also is a God of love and mercy. Repeatedly the writings of the prophets reaffirm this fact. The house of Israel fell before the judgments of God because of iniquity and rebellion. In the last days they will be gathered again and become glorious because of his mercy and love. We, living in the last days, are the recipients of that mercy and love. Therefore, our own spiritual roots sink deep into the fertile soil of the Old Testament. Indeed, the vision and perspective supplied by the great men and women who wrote therein provides a depth and breadth of understanding not found elsewhere.

3

The Covenant People

As Israel stood ready to enter the land promised to them through Abraham more than four centuries before, Moses delivered one of his last urgent messages. He knew his ministry was to close shortly. This was to be one of his final sermons. His purpose was to impress the Israelites with a sense of their importance as the covenant people. To do this, he reviewed their recent history in this dramatic way:

> For ask now of the days that are past, which were before thee, since the day that God created man upon the earth, and ask from the one side of heaven unto the other, whether there has been any such thing as this. . . .
>
> Did ever people hear the voice of God speaking out of the midst of the fire, as thou hast heard, and live?
>
> Or hath God assayed to go and take him a nation from the midst of another nation, by temptations, by signs, and

by wonders, and by war, and by a mighty hand, and by a stretched out arm, and by great terrors, according to all that the Lord your God did for you in Egypt before your eyes?

And because he loved thy fathers, therefore he chose their seed after them, and brought thee out in his sight with his mighty power out of Egypt;

To drive out nations from before thee greater and mightier than thou art, to bring thee in, to give thee their land for an inheritance, as it is this day. (Deuteronomy 4:32-34, 37-38; italics added.)

In another sermon given shortly after this one, Moses commanded them to remember that

thou art an holy people unto the Lord thy God: the Lord *thy God hath chosen thee to be a special people unto himself, above all people that are on the face of the earth.*

The Lord did not set his love upon you, nor choose you, because ye were more in number than any people; for ye were fewest of all people:

But because the Lord loved you, and because he would keep the oath which he had sworn unto your fathers, hath the Lord . . . redeemed you [from Egypt]. . . .

Wherefore it shall come to pass, if ye hearken to these judgments, and keep, and do them, that the Lord *thy God shall keep unto thee the covenant and the mercy which he sware unto thy fathers.* (Deuteronomy 7:6-8, 12; italics added.)

From this we see that Israel's favored position at that time was not due to any acts on her own part, but rather to the promises which the Lord had established with Abraham, Isaac, and Jacob. These promises were actually no more than the extension of promises given to more ancient patriarchs such as Seth and Noah, and they established the doctrine of election. This doctrine, as explained by Brigham Young and Willard Richards, shows "that God has chosen or elected certain individuals to certain blessings, or to the performance of certain works." (*HC* 4:258.) This election was based upon their works in the premortal existence. It was there that the chosen race or house of Israel was organized.

Eligibility into this lineage was dependent upon individual behavior. Elder Bruce R. McConkie has pointed out that "in this prior life . . . we developed various capacities and talents. Some developed them in one field and some in another. The most important of all fields was the field of spirituality—the ability, the talent, the capacity to recognize truth." ("When Thou Art Converted, Strengthen Thy Brethren," *Study Guide for Melchizedek Priesthood Quorums of the Church 1974-75* [Salt Lake City: The Church of Jesus Christ of Latter-day Saints, 1974], pages 8-9.) There were some who misused their opportunity to learn:

> God gave his children their free agency even in the spirit world, by which the individual spirits had the privilege, just as men have here, of choosing the good and rejecting the evil, or partaking of the evil to suffer the consequences of their sins. Because of this, some even there were more faithful than others in keeping the commandments of the Lord. Some were of greater intelligence than others, as we find it here, and were honored accordingly. . . .
>
> The spirits of men had their free agency, some were greater than others, and from among them the Father called and foreordained his prophets and rulers. Jeremiah and Abraham were two of them. [Jeremiah 1:5; Abraham 3:23.] *The spirits of men were not equal. They may have had an equal start* [Alma 13:5-7], and we know they were all innocent in the beginning [D&C 93:38]; but the right of free agency which was given to them enabled some to outstrip others, and thus, through the eons of immortal existence, to become more intelligent, more faithful, for they were free to act for themselves, to think for themselves, to receive the truth or rebel against it. (Joseph Fielding Smith, *Doctrines of Salvation*,

comp. Bruce R. McConkie, 3 vols. [Salt Lake City: Bookcraft, 1954-56], 1:58-59.)

It was from those who had properly used their agency
that the chosen lineage was organized and its members were
foreordained to the mission they were to accomplish in
mortality. It was this premortal status to which Moses
alluded when, during his last discourse to Israel, he stated:

> Remember the days of old, consider the years of many
> generations: ask thy father, and he will shew thee; thy
> elders, and they will tell thee.
> When the most High divided to the nations their inherit-
> ance, when he separated the sons of Adam, *he set the bounds
> of the people according to the number of the children of Israel.*
> For the Lord's portion is his people; Jacob is the lot of
> his inheritance. (Deuteronomy 32:7-9; italics added.)

Abraham, as with Seth, Shem, and others, received the
promise that these elect spirits would be born into mortality
as his posterity. It would be his descendants that would
have the right to the gospel and to the priesthood, with the
responsibility of its administration, whenever this was
upon the earth. This promise assured Abraham that at least
a remnant of his posterity would continue through to the
end of time.

Being born into the elect race, however, does not
assure any individual that he will obtain eternal life. Joseph
Smith stressed that unconditional election to eternal life
from before the foundation of the world was not a correct
doctrine: "God did elect or predestinate, that all those who
would be saved, should be saved in Christ Jesus . . . but
He passes over no man's sins, but visits them with correc-
tion, and if His children will not repent of their sins He will
discard them." (*HC*, 4:360.)

The history of Israel proves the correctness of this teaching. Many, after proving their valiancy in the first estate and thereby being guaranteed access to the greatest blessings which God could grant to mortal man, rejected these blessings during the trials of the second estate. Through rebellion and following after the lusts of the flesh they were rejected by God, and they forfeited the spiritual blessings he had in store for them. In fact, the history of Israel can be viewed as a series of descents from the great spiritual heights achieved by the first patriarchs, to a low point from about 400 B.C. to the ministry of John the Baptist. During this time Israel's relationship with God was tenuous, at best. It will be the purpose of this chapter to explore these descents and their consequences on the covenant people. The story is not all gloom. There are a number of bright spots which reveal the spiritual power and close association with God that can be achieved when an individual or people refuse to yield to the flesh and the ways of the fallen world.

PRE-FLOOD

Generally when the history of the earth from Adam to Noah is considered, most are conscious of the deep and widespread spiritual filthiness to which the people descended and which ended only when the earth was cleansed by the great Flood. It also should be remembered, however, that during that time men rose to the greatest spiritual heights ever achieved in earth's history. As wickedness began to spread, Adam took definite steps to combat it. He preached the gospel and sought to bring his children into the presence of God. About 325 years after the Fall, Adam

commissioned his grandson Enos to gather the righteous
and establish them in a land of promise. This Enos succeeded in doing, naming the land after his son Cainan. So
successful was he that 350 years later peace and righteousness were still abounding. From this land missionaries
were continually sent to preach the gospel and gather all
who would hearken. (See Moses 6:17, 23, 41.)

It was in this land that Enoch was born. When he was
about sixty-five years old the powers of heaven descended
upon him and he became a mighty seer unto whom even the
mountains and rivers were in subjection. He initially was
commissioned to warn the unrighteous of the coming day of
judgment and to proclaim repentance. But few listened.
Great wars began to ravage the land. The righteous were
attacked. (See Moses 7:5, 6, 13, 16.) As a means of defense,
Enoch led the righteous to a land that became a place of
refuge and a Zion. Adam must have dwelt near there after
the Fall, because we commonly are taught that Enoch's
Zion and Adam's valley of Adam-ondi-Ahman were near
each other in what is now Missouri. It was in Adam-ondi-
Ahman that Adam held a great council in which he bestowed upon his righteous children their patriarchal blessings. In glorious vision, he unfolded to them the entire
history of the earth, making known the works of God in
every dispensation. (See D&C 107:53-57.)

Adam called the council because of his desire to bring
his posterity into the presence of God. (See *TPJS*, pages
158-59.) Enoch had already been successful in establishing
the foundations of a city of holiness called Zion. Upon this
place the glory of the Lord was present in such power that
its enemies would not come near. Adam's desire was even
greater than that, however. He sought to bring his posterity

into a city whose builder and maker was God. (See *TPJS*, page 159.) Because he died three years after this council, he did not live to see his wish come true, but some of his posterity continued to dwell in such righteousness that about 125 years later Zion, the city of Enoch, was taken into heaven. (See Moses 7:68-69.)

This high point of spiritual perfection established the possibility of a goal which holy men and prophets have sought since those days. (See D&C 45:12.) This is the background of the urgent teachings, pleadings and warnings of such prophets as Moses, Elijah, Jeremiah and Isaiah, just to name a few. They sought to establish Zion but were unable to because of the wickedness of their people. They received a promise, however, that they would find Zion and see it in the flesh. (See D&C 45:13-14.)

COVENANT LINE CONTINUED THROUGH FLOOD

When God took Zion into heaven, he did not leave the earth without a warning voice. Methuselah, Lamech and Noah combined ministries to seek out those who would repent and come to God. Those who did so with full purpose of heart were translated and joined the people of Enoch. (See Inspired Version, Genesis 14:32-33; Moses 7:27.)

Continual segregation of the righteous from the wicked soon removed that element of the society which acted to retard the advance of evil. The lack of opposition allowed those remaining to have free expression of their corrupt wills until "every man was lifted up in the imagination of the thoughts of his heart, being only evil continually" (Moses 8:22). In their wickedness they sought the lives of the last who opposed them. Noah was able to escape, but "his heart was pained" because they would not turn from their depravity. (See Moses 8:25.) Having obtained the First Presidency by which he held dominion over every creature (see *TPJS*, page 157) and reigned as supreme patriarch over the earth (see Abraham 1:19), he besought God to cleanse the earth from its great iniquity. (See Moses 8:25-26.) God responded to the righteous desires and great sorrow of this holy man and sent the floods to baptize and cleanse the earth.

The Flood came as no surprise to the righteous. For over one thousand years the prophets knew of it and warned the people. During that time preparations were made to preserve the covenant race. Methuselah, the son of Enoch, was commissioned to stay behind when Zion was translated so that he could preserve that lineage upon the earth. (See Moses 8:2.) To his son, Lamech, Noah was born. With Noah, God established the covenant which had belonged to the patriarchs down to his day (Genesis 6:18). This was passed on to Shem, from whom Abraham was descended.

ABRAHAM, ANCESTOR OF COVENANT PEOPLE

The seeds of apostasy came through the Flood mainly in the family of Ham, though some found fertile ground to grow in all of Noah's posterity. There were some who resisted the influence of apostasy, however. Among these was Melchizedek, who was approved of God and received the holy priesthood "after the order of the covenant which God made with Enoch, it being after the order of the Son of God." (Inspired Version, Genesis 14:27-28.) By the time Abraham was born, Melchizedek ruled as king of

Salem, city of peace. At the time he assumed the throne "his people had waxed strong in iniquity and abomination; yea, they had all gone astray." (Alma 13:17.) Melchizedek began to labor among them, however, preaching repentance and establishing righteousness. He was so effective that he brought order and peace to his kingdom and purity and holiness as well. The development of his kingdom closely approximated that of Zion, about which they knew; and "men having this faith, coming up unto this order [of the priesthood] of God, were translated and taken up into heaven." (Inspired Version, Genesis 14:32-33.)

Again, it was necessary for some of the righteous to remain behind that the covenant line might continue. One of those who remained was Abraham. Though he met the great king of Salem, he was not permitted to enter into his kingdom. "By faith he sojourned in the land of promise, as in a strange country, dwelling in tabernacles with Isaac and Jacob, the heirs with him of the same promise: For he looked for a city which hath foundations, whose builder and maker is God." (Hebrews 11:9-10; see also Bruce R. McConkie, *Doctrinal New Testament Commentary*, 3 vols. [Salt Lake City: Bookcraft, 1965-73], 3:200-203.) Indeed, when the Lord established the covenant with him he said, "And remember the covenant which I make with thee; for it shall be an everlasting covenant; and thou shalt remember the days of Enoch thy father." (Inspired Version, Genesis 13:13.)

True to his commission, Abraham yielded to the will of the Lord. Over the length and breadth of the land he traveled, preaching and winning souls to God. Ur, Haran, Canaan, and Egypt heard his voice. But he did not enter the holy kingdom of Melchizedek which was taken into heaven.

He had to look to a latter day when the foundations of a new and glorious Zion would be laid within the confines of his eternal inheritance. For his courage and faithfulness he received this plaudit from God: "For I know him, that he will command his children and his household after him, and they shall keep the way of the Lord." (Genesis 18:19.) This blood that flows through the veins of all who are of the chosen lineage is the blood of the patriarchs all the way back to Adam. It is shared by all the tribes of Israel. Little wonder that Abraham was chosen to preserve the covenant and to be the father of those who enter therein.

Before Abraham's day the very righteous hoped to enter into a Zion of the Lord and be translated. That is what happened to the people of Enoch's city before the Flood. After the Flood apparently many went into heaven with Melchizedek's city, Salem. The purposes of the Lord would not be fulfilled if every righteous person was taken into heaven, however. We are here to be tested and tried. Apparently there are many whose premortal performance suggests terrestrial or telestial status and who have to obtain bodies and go through an experience that will demonstrate what they really desire. Therefore, from Abraham's day on down, translation has been a rare experience for even the most righteous. In that sense, the opportunities for the covenant people were somewhat lessened after Melchizedek's day. Most of Noah's descendants were not even worthy of enjoying the benefits of the gospel.

COVENANT PEOPLE IN EGYPT AND WILDERNESS

The ascent of Jacob's youngest son, Joseph, to the second highest position in the Egyptian government was not due to chance. As he well knew, he owed his position to the divine gifts which had been bestowed upon him. These gifts were not given to him only because of his righteousness; they were necessary for God to fulfill his plans to preserve Israel. Because of Joseph's favored position he was able to secure one of the choicest locations in all Egypt for his family —the land of Goshen. (See Genesis 47:6.) Here the children of Israel multiplied until they became more numerous and mightier than the Egyptians. Fearing that Israel might aid or become an enemy, Egypt forced her into the bitter affliction of slavery. Yet the chosen people continued to multiply. Eventually, the Egyptians sought to slow the Hebrew birthrate by destroying all male babies. The God-fearing midwives found devious ways to save some. One of these was Moses.

The career of Moses is fascinating. His mother was successful in getting him placed under the watchful eye of Pharaoh's daughter by the stratagem of placing him in a watertight basket and letting it float down the Nile into the area where Pharaoh's daughter and her court were bathing. From then on his mother was able to raise him without fear until he had grown enough to enter the security of Pharaoh's house. There he distinguished himself as a great military commander, until his siding with the Hebrews brought him under Pharaoh's wrath. After fleeing Egypt, Moses married the eldest daughter of Jethro, the priest of Midian.

The Midianites apparently were descendants of Abraham through his wife Keturah. (See Genesis 25:1-4.) The priesthood of Jethro descended from a prophet by the name of Esaias who was a contemporary of Abraham. (D&C 84:7-13.) It was from this line that Moses was ordained. That there was such an alternate line of authority is indicative of the foreknowledge of God. At the moment God was ready to bring Israel out of Egypt with power, the priesthood, through this other line, was there; and Moses was schooled in the priesthood and ready for his assignment.

Commissioned by God, Moses went back to the land of Egypt. There he was successful in freeing the Hebrews from bondage and leading them to the gates of the promised land. All this, however, was with great difficulty and heart-ache. His ministry marks another spiritual descent of the covenant race. It was his desire, as with Adam before him, to bring the chosen people into the presence of God. (See *TPJS*, page 159; D&C 84:23, 24.) When God sought to establish his covenant with them at Sinai, they rebelled. They rejected not only Zion but the gospel as well. For this, God swore they would not be allowed to receive his glory while in the wilderness. By and by he took the mighty and holy Moses from their midst. With him went the higher priesthood (D&C 84:25-26). From that time on, only the prophets and, perhaps, a few others held the Melchizedek Priesthood. The Lord did not abandon the Hebrews, however. Because of his mercy and the covenant made with the ancients, he gave Israel the lesser or Levitical Priest-hood and a lesser law. This lesser law was designed to remind them of the Savior and to lead them closer to him. (See Galatians 3:24.)

Without the higher priesthood and its ordinances, Israel was barred from receiving the power of godliness (D&C 84:19-24). Without this power, Zion could not be achieved (D&C 105:4, 11-12, 36-37). Barred from Zion and without the gospel possessed by Abraham, the covenant people were yet another step lower in their spiritual regres-sion. They were not abandoned, however. As Moses gathered Israel about him shortly before his translation, he proclaimed there was still hope. God had been with them for the forty years in the wilderness. There he had provided food and water. What's more, he preserved them with miracles for the whole time: "Your clothes are not waxen old upon you, and thy shoe is not waxen old upon thy foot." (Deuteronomy 29:5.) Now as they were about to enter the promised land they were promised that God would continue to be with them. If they turned to him in the last days, he would not "forget the covenant of thy fathers which he sware unto them." (Deuteronomy 4:29-31.) In the meantime, they could, if faithful, enjoy great blessings even without Zion and while in the midst of their enemies. (See Leviticus 26 and Deuteronomy 28.)

COVENANT PEOPLE ESTABLISHED
IN PROMISED LAND

Shortly after Moses' last attempt to awaken Israel to her potential, he was taken out of their midst. He was translated and, no doubt, allowed to enter the glory of that great city whose builder and founder was God and which he had sought during his ministry. Meanwhile, Joshua was left with the struggle of trying to keep spiritually weak Israel worthy to maintain the newer and lesser covenant she now had. The total possession of the promised land was critical if the Hebrews were to ever achieve the degree of holiness necessary to obtain the blessings promised by Moses. (See Leviticus 26 and Deuteronomy 28.) Therefore, the Lord was strict with how they were to proceed:

> Then ye shall drive out all the inhabitants of the land from before you, and destroy all their pictures, and destroy all their molten images, and quite pluck down their high places:

> And ye shall dispossess the inhabitants of the land, and
> dwell therein. . . . (Numbers 33:52-53.)

The consequences of disobedience he also made perfectly
clear:

> But if ye will not drive out the inhabitants of the land from
> before you; then it shall come to pass, that those which ye
> let remain of them shall be pricks in your eyes, and thorns
> in your sides, and shall vex you in the land wherein ye dwell.
> (Numbers 33:55.)

The Lord was against any association between the
Canaanites and Hebrews because of the extremely vile
nature of the pagan Canaanite religious practices. The
Canaanites had become depraved, hardened, and corrupt to
the point that when the word of the Lord was preached
among them they utterly refused to repent. (See 1 Nephi
17:32-35.) This was so despite their full knowledge of the
power that attended the Hebrews in crossing the Red Sea
and destroying the Amorite armies in the Transjordan. This
led one Canaanite to proclaim: "The Lord your God, he is
God in heaven above, and in earth beneath" (Joshua 2:9-
11). Yet, in spite of this, the people of the land clung to
their idols. Though they feared when news reached them of
Joshua parting the Jordan during the flood season and the
Hebrews crossing into Palestine on dry ground, they would
not turn from their abominations. (See Joshua 5:1.) No
wonder the wrath of the Lord was finally kindled against
them and "did curse the land against them, and bless it unto
our fathers." (1 Nephi 17:35.)

The Israelites were not obedient to the Lord, however.
Almost from the outset they began to compromise themselves: They retained idols, they did not pluck down the
high places and the groves, and they even made a league
with some of the inhabitants of the land. Joshua continually

admonished the people to do as God had directed. Only if they did so would they be able to possess the land and be totally secure against destruction themselves. Because they would not obey, Joshua finally warned them:

> Know for a certainty that the Lord your God will no more drive out any of these nations from before you; but they shall be snares and traps unto you, and scourges in your sides, and thorns in your eyes, until ye perish from off this good land which the Lord your God hath given you. (Joshua 23:13.)

And so Israel never found peace and rest in her promised land. Except for a brief respite under Solomon, she was at war continually.

WHY GOD GAVE ISRAEL JUDGES

During the reign of the judges, Israel ceased to act as a united front. There was cooperation between individual tribes at times, but for the most part each acted independently in meeting its enemies. One of the most important battles took place between five of the tribes of Israel and the forces of Jabin, "King of the Canaanites," under the direction of his general, Sisera. The iron chariots of the Canaanites posed a real threat to Israel's ability to wage a successful war against these people who held the northern territory. Nevertheless, the Israelite forces attacked under the inspiration of Deborah and Barak. From their vantage point on Mount Tabor, Deborah and Barak directed their army and successfully routed the enemy. (See Judges 4, 5.) This defeat marked the end of Canaanite domination.

In addition to fighting the local inhabitants, Israel continually had to ward off invasion. The primary threat during the reign of the judges came from the local neighbors. Ehud was successful in driving Moab out of Jericho (Judges 3:12-30). Gideon used a handful of men in a night raid which successfully terrified bedouin conquerors out of the rich Jezreel Valley which they had held for seven years (Judges 6, 7). Jephthah was triumphant in leading an army against intruding Ammonites on the east side of the Jordan (Judges 11), and Samson harassed the Philistines in an attempt to keep them out of the territory of Dan (Judges 13-16). In spite of their growing apostasy, it was in each case the power of the Lord, Israel's King, acting through these people, that brought victory. (See, for example, Judges 6:23; 14:19.)

The book of Judges reveals extremely low moral standards, which were caused by many of the Hebrews adopting Canaanite idolatry. Nevertheless, there were some who were faithful. When many in Israel wanted a mortal king that she might be like the other nations, one such faithful one (Gideon) refused (Judges 8). The theocratic ideal was best, and as long as God was Israel's King he was bound to defend her. Many Israelites did not understand this, however, and so the refrain for an earthly king continued. What they did not seem to realize was that the high degree of personal freedom in which "every man did that which was right in his own eyes" (Judges 17:6) was a direct result of living under a theocratic government. Compared to later times, the reign of the judges was a high-water mark of freedom and righteousness.

Toward the end of the reign of the judges the prophet-judge Samuel began his ministry. He succeeded in reclaiming many Hebrews to the true worship of Jehovah at Mizpeh (1 Samuel 7). He led Israel in thwarting an unexpected attack by the Philistines and then went on to help them regain territory which had been lost. But in spite of his prophetic power and military prowess, Israel still demanded a king. Heartsick, Samuel took their petition to the Lord.

ISRAEL REJECTS DIVINE KING FOR MORTAL ONE

Samuel initially mistook Israel's desire as a personal rejection, but the Lord soon revealed to him its true significance: "They have not rejected thee, but they have rejected me, that I should not reign over them" (1 Samuel 8:7).

In refusing to be ruled by God through his judges, Israel took yet another step in her spiritual descent. Even so, there was still a tie to God. As long as the king was appointed by the Lord and would hearken to the voice of prophetic authority, God could still lead Israel. But if ever the king refused to listen, God would no longer rule. At this point the bonds of the already tenuous covenant would be severed. The result would be the forfeiture by Israel of the right to remain in the promised land. Of this Moses had already warned them centuries before when he declared that when the covenant was broken "ye shall soon perish from off the land. . . . And the Lord shall scatter you among the nations." (Deuteronomy 4:26-27.) The consequences being so great it is not surprising that Samuel would first warn Israel before granting her the desire for a mortal king. (See 1 Samuel 8:10-18.) Despite his efforts, Israel chose to have a king.

Samuel was led to anoint Saul. Saul's reign showed how hard it is to be a righteous king. Though he valiantly defended the Hebrews at Jabesh-Gilead (1 Samuel 11:1-13) and was even generous to those who opposed his rule, he soon usurped priesthood authority which brought upon him the condemnation of God. This he did in offering sacrifices in preparation for battle with the Philistines because he had become impatient waiting for Samuel to appear and do it. (1 Samuel 13.) Unfortunately, Samuel's rebuke did not serve to curb his growing arrogance. In defiance of a direct commandment from God, Saul refused to utterly exterminate the Amalekites and their flocks. He saved the king and the best animals. For this he was finally rejected by God, and Samuel was sent secretly to anoint David in his place. (See 1 Samuel 15, 16.)

From that point on, the fortunes of Saul waned. Indecision and behavior bordering on madness marked his last years. He allowed the Philistines to penetrate far into Israelite territory. In a vain attempt to drive them out he was killed at Mt. Gilboa. Abner, his captain, was successful in reassembling the beaten army east of the Jordan (1 Samuel 31). With what little power remained, Ishbosheth, Saul's son, succeeded in establishing a brief kingship in Gilead. Meanwhile, David had been successful in winning the southern tribes of Judah and Benjamin to his banner at Hebron. For the next two years, skirmishes and intrigue marred the relationship between the two factions, finally bringing about the downfall of both Abner and Ishbosheth. Then a relieved Israel united under David.

Once firmly in control, David took the initiative. He needed a capital which was more centrally located, not only for better administration but also to placate the northern tribes who were jealous of the importance given to the southern capital of Hebron. The Jebusite city of Jerusalem looked promising and soon fell to David's army. The Philistines feared the consolidation of Israel and therefore sent her armies against David. He met them at Rephaim and so thoroughly defeated them that they ceased to pose any real threat to Israel throughout his reign. As a general he was unexcelled, and he succeeded in subjugating the territory from the Egyptian border to the northern Euphrates. Tribute from Edom, Moab, Ammon and areas beyond the Sea of Galilee filled his treasure. (See 2 Samuel 8.)

During his reign David made Jerusalem the focal point of the nation. This he did by fortifying the city, building a palace and an administrative center, and bringing the ark of the covenant from Shiloh to Jerusalem. David wished to use his fortunes to build the house of the Lord. This he was not permitted to do, though he was allowed to gather the materials after the floor plan had been revealed (1 Chronicles 22). Though outwardly successful, David's family and court were wrought with dissension. His sinful conduct in the case of Uriah and Bathsheba served to estrange him from God, and family intrigue brought him much sorrow. His preference for Solomon, a son of Bathsheba, over his older sons led to revolt. Absalom, one of these sons, even succeeded in temporarily taking Jerusalem, though he was killed by Joab in battle shortly thereafter (2 Samuel 15-18).

There were disloyalty and insurrection among the northern tribes during David's last years. The majority of the people, however, seemed to have always sided with this brilliant king to the point that even when opportunity presented itself, Israel's neighbors refused to engage her in war. The reign of David, though full of shortcomings, was the best Israel would know. Though personally weakened through tragic sin, David led Israel in the way of the Lord. It was to God that he continually turned his thoughts in both victory and defeat. Even prophetic rebuke did not cause him to turn from God. In this is seen the true greatness of the man.

Solomon did not have the magnanimity of his father, nor was he as considerate of the financial burden of government. Though he was endowed with great wisdom and with spiritual gifts, he was not loyal to God for long. Once secure on the throne, he set about to accomplish the major aims of his reign: the building of the temple, the consolidation of the kingdom, and the development of a vast and efficient bureaucracy to serve the gluttonous desires of pomp and power. For all this, the requisite human wisdom was given. A navy was built, trade expanded, and riches as never before poured into the kingdom. Foreign craftsmen and merchants from all over the Near East, as well as diplomats and visitors, gave Jerusalem a cosmopolitan atmosphere.

There were drawbacks, however. The grandiose building enterprises, the army and navy, all required revenue and manpower. To get these, taxes were laid upon the people in terms of both time and money. Continued success compounded the need. The administrative staff grew. Payments in kind required the building and fortifying of store cities. All the while the royal household was expanding. Taxes increased with little sign of relief. It is no wonder that there was increased discontent, especially among the poor. Israel's traditions were foreign to supporting the indulgences of an oriental royal house. The pressure of this heavy bureaucratic structure began to crack the foundations of unity.

A greater danger than this financial burden threatened the solidarity and strength of the nation. The king who had worked so hard to build the house of the Lord turned to practices which denied the very purpose of that temple. In blatant disregard for the law and the prophetic voice, he began to worship idols of stone, wood, and metal (1 Kings 1:2-5). Israel had wanted a king and so received one. In so doing, she had entrusted to one man too much of the care of the covenant. The weaknesses of Solomon started Israel's slide to her next lower level of retreat from the Zion that once could have been. The only thing that would save her from extermination was the grace of God and the promises made to the fathers.

BROKEN COVENANT, BROKEN NATION

Before the death of Solomon, signs of rebellion began to appear in the kingdom. Edom and Moab were preparing for revolt. The youthful Jeroboam, an official from the tribe of Ephraim, took advantage of his position to gain popularity and encourage rebellion. Solomon learned of his ambitions and ordered his execution. Jeroboam fled to Egypt to escape. (See 1 Kings 11.) When Solomon died, his son Rehoboam took the throne. Rehoboam was insensitive to the growing discontent of the masses. Listening to his youthful cohorts rather than the older diplomats, he tried to initiate further repressive measures. This cost him the support of the ten northern tribes, who made Jeroboam their king and split the kingdom in two. (1 Kings 12.) From the beginning, Jeroboam showed little concern for the Lord and led his people into an idolatrous perversion of the law of Moses. Within two hundred years, the Northern Kingdom would go into captivity and would be lost to the ancient world.

Initially there was rivalry between the two kingdoms. To reduce the powerful pull of Jerusalem on those who expressed a desire to worship after the manner of the law, Jeroboam set up golden calf shrines at Dan and Bethel and told the people they could sacrifice there instead of at the temple in Jerusalem. Corrupt priests and Levites accepted the positions offered them there. The spiritual insensitivity of the people allowed them to rationalize the wickedness of the idolatrous images that were a part of their Egyptian past.

After nearly fifty years of hostility, the kingdoms of Israel (sometimes called the northern or ten tribes kingdom) and Judah (generally considered the tribes of Judah, Benjamin and Levi, although Simeon seems to have been absorbed into Judah) formed an alliance and all rivalry ceased. Israel established a new and beautiful capital at Samaria. Under the administrative excellence of her successive kings, Israel became wealthy. She gained international status and prestige which brought her to the attention of the growing Assyrian nation to the north and east. But all the while she was sinking further into spiritual wickedness. Under Ahab and his Phoenecian wife, Jezebel, all forms of Jehovah worship were abolished and the sensual practices of Baal became widespread. Throughout this entire period the warning voices of the prophets were heard. Eventually, Elijah openly confronted the Baal worshippers and with a unique display of divine power was able to weaken their hold. (See 1 Kings 18.) But this did not last.

During this time the united forces of both kingdoms temporarily were able to bring Edom and Moab back under subjection. But Israel was continually under pressure from Syria, which she was able to keep back only with a large and expensive army. Fortunately, Israel was rich enough to support such an army as well as an expansive building campaign. But the wealth being generated only benefitted the upper classes. Generally, the large poor class was suppressed and exploited by the aristocrats.

With wealth, power, and corruption increasing at the top, it is not surprising that kings were overthrown. Jehu was one who succeeded in doing this. He won the army and probably the common people to his side, overthrew the old dynasty, and began a new one—the longest Israel would know. (See 2 Kings 9, 10.) One of his first acts was to purge the land of Baal worshippers. He destroyed the entire family of Ahab and Jezebel and slaughtered many others who would not turn from the practice. His zeal, however, did not seem to stem from a genuine concern for Jehovah. More likely he was attempting to win the favor of the many anti-Baal factions. His efforts did not succeed. Instead, they only served to weaken the country to the point that it was unable to withstand the advances of Syria, who was about to take the Israelite territory east of the Jordan and a portion of the rich Jezreel Valley and coastal plains (2 Kings 10:32-33; 12:7). Israel was saved from possibly becoming a part of the Syrian kingdom by the successful invasion of Assyria into that land.

With the pressure removed, Jeroboam II was able to reassert Israel's authority over the lost territory. He expanded trade, enriched the land owners and amassed a fortune for the royal house. But again the wealth only benefitted the rich. The common people continued in poverty because of taxes and usury. This was indicative of the spiritually bankrupt condition of the state. The people as a whole had become selfish and uncaring. Though the worship of Jehovah through sacrificial ordinances was again popular, the total disregard for the heart of the Mosaic law

brought forth censure from such prophets as Amos and
Hosea. They saw the social injustices for what they really
were—outward manifestations of the deepest estrangement
from God. Though they pleaded with Israel to repent while
there was yet time, the burden of their message was war,
destruction, and captivity. Israel's prosperity and freedom from her enemies were only a brief respite. If she
refused to turn to God, her iniquity would be full and she
would fall.

Despite the growing turmoil and insecurity which
began to plague the nation, the people did not respond to
such messages of doom. The royal house itself was in a
state of turbulance. Within thirteen years, three kings were
assassinated as various men made bids for the throne.
Vacillation, indecision and, eventually, wrong choices
marked Israel's foreign policy. This proved disastrous.
Adopting an anti-Assyrian policy, she tried to force the
kingdom of Judah into an alliance. In a partial response
to Judah's plea Assyria marched against Israel and took a
number of towns and many prisoners. After Assyria's
withdrawal, Israel's last king ascended the throne, after
assassinating his predecessor. He continued the anti-
Assyrian policy, refusing to pay the tribute which guaranteed nominal freedom. Such action brought quick retalia-
tion. Assyria returned with an occupying army, beseiged
Samaria for three years, and captured and finally deported
the nation's population. (See 2 Kings 15, 17.) The dire
prophecies of Amos and Hosea were now fact.

Judah did not fall with the Northern Kingdom. There
were at least two major reasons for this. Situated as she
was in the southern highlands, she was both less prosperous
and less vulnerable to the northern powers than her sister

kingdom. These things combined to make her less attractive to would-be conquerors. But the major reason seems to be that Judah did not abandon righteousness as rapidly as did the Northern Kingdom. Having the temple and the true priests of Levi in her midst helped retard any mass abandonment of the Mosaic traditions. But another factor also assisted. As the Northern Kingdom abandoned itself to idolatry, many of the more righteous Hebrews left to take up residence in Judah. This was especially true of the righteous Levites. (Perhaps many of the more wicked were attracted out of the Southern Kingdom also.)

Thus, Judah became the home of some from all the tribes of Israel. Therefore, in 600 B.C. we find Lehi, a Manassehite, and Ishmael, an Ephraimite, dwelling in the land of Jerusalem (Alma 10:3; *Journal of Discourses*, 26 vols. [London: Latter-day Saints' Book Depot, 1854-86], 23:184; hereafter cited as *JD*.) The population was always predominately that of the tribe of Judah, however, Benjamin and Levi making up the next largest group. Through this intermingling of the tribes, combined with cross-tribal marriages, the tribal identity became less and less important. Though we speak of ten tribes being led away, there is no doubt that some of Judah, Benjamin, and Levi went with them. On the other hand, at least some members of all of the other tribes remained behind. This conglomeration of people gathered in the south, though conscious of their ancestry, accepted the generic title of Judah and would someday be known only as Jews.

Though initially less stormy than her sister nation, Judah's history was not without internal violence, intrigue, and eventual disaster. During the ninth century B.C., pagan influences began to increase in the land. Because of the occasional reforms initiated by rulers such as Asa and Joash, these never gained the hold that they did in the Northern Kingdom (1 Kings 15; 2 Kings 11). During the eighth century B.C. Judah experienced increased prosperity, as did Israel. Under King Uzziah, Jerusalem was strongly fortified, the army was built up, and neighboring people were subdued. It was at this time that Isaiah and Micah began their ministries. They were late contemporaries of Amos and Hosea who were working in the north. This was the time of the continued encroachments of Assyria into Palestine. When Israel adopted its anti-Assyrian policy, became leagued with Syria, and threatened to force Judah to join this alliance, her king, rejecting the council of Isaiah (see Isaiah 7), appealed to Assyria. This resulted in Israel becoming a tributary of the great power. It did buy Judah a little time; but she did not use it wisely. King Hezekiah, again refusing to listen to Isaiah, was enticed by Egypt and Ashdod to join in rebelling against Assyria. The result was a crushing Assyrian invasion. The prospects of this army taking and perhaps sacking the holy city brought Hezekiah to his senses, and he humbled himself before the Lord in fasting and prayer. Word came through Isaiah that his prayer was heard. Shortly thereafter a devastating plague hit the Assyrian army, forcing its withdrawal (2 Kings 19:35). Thus, Judah was spared for another hundred years.

The good accomplished by Hezekiah was reversed by the next two kings. As they adopted the cult and mode of the Assyrians, idolatry began to increase among the upper class. Protests from the prophets led to bloodshed. Nevertheless, these fearless men continued to warn. Zephaniah was successful in winning the ear of Josiah, who instituted an effective reformation. The decline in Assyrian power augmented his labors. It was at this time that Jeremiah responded to a divine call and began his ministry. Coinciding with this, the book of the law was discovered in the temple. All these things combined to add impetus to the reform. Unfortunately, the outward improvements were not reaching into the hearts of the people. The worship of Jehovah was nothing more than a facade covering avarice, greed, corruption, and sensuality. Jeremiah rebuked the people for their wickedness. If they did not turn to the Lord with full purpose of heart, he warned, their end would be no better than Israel's. (Jeremiah 9, 13.)

In 609 B.C. Babylon, which had conquered Assyria, descended into the area, insisting on allegiance. To assure cooperation, Nebuchadnezzar took hostages and returned to his capital. Among those taken into Babylon was Ezekiel and later young Daniel. This close call with disaster did not serve to bring Judah to repentance. Jeremiah's insistence that doom could not be averted cost him suffering and imprisonment. Though he tried to warn Judah that flirting with Egypt would bring disaster, the leaders would not listen. Finally, in response to her disloyalty, Nebuchadnezzar launched his armies.

In 587 B.C. Jerusalem fell after a long and bloody siege. Over the next few years Judah's entire population, with the exception of some of the very poor living in a scattered condition in the hills, was deported. As with Israel, Judah could blame no one but herself for the disaster. Warned and rewarned, she would not return to full obedience to the covenant. But as black as things were, hope was not entirely lost. Jeremiah promised that the Jews would return from Babylon in seventy years and rebuild the temple. From that day until recent times, however, there has never been a free and independent Jewish state in Palestine. Judah had lost the covenant land until the latter days.

COVENANT, CAPTIVITY, AND RETURN

Though Judah had abandoned God, God had not abandoned Judah. In her captivity he watched over her. Daniel became a prominent leader through divine design and was instrumental in protecting his people. Later, Esther became queen and was in a position to save the Jews from planned extinction. But this was not the only place God manifested himself. Through his prophets—Jeremiah, Ezekiel, Daniel and others—he held out hope for a renewal of the covenant, a return to the promised land, a partial restoration of national autonomy, and a rebuilding of the temple. This was not because his people deserved it, but was to fulfill promises to the fathers that the promised people would be saved and the Savior would be born to the house of David. (See Ezekiel 11:16-20; 36:21-28.)

After seventy years of captivity, as Jeremiah prophesied (Jeremiah 25:11), the promises began to be fulfilled. The Babylonian Empire fell to the Persians in 538 B.C. Cyrus, the new emperor, was able to conquer the entire Middle East and intitiate a policy of returning exiled peoples to their own lands and allowing them to worship as they willed. Many, though not a majority, of the Jews took advantage of this situation to return to their homeland.

The years that had passed saw the Jews scattered over most of the Near East. Yet the experience had worked a miracle. In at least three respects the Jews that came out of captivity were different than the Baal-worshipping divisive people they had been. First, they never again returned to image worship; gone forever were idols of stone, wood, and metal. Second, the law became very important to them; in fact, they tended to make it their new idol. Jewish intellectuals, the forerunners of the rabbis, arose and began to take interest in collecting, codifying, and canonizing the books of the Bible. These they came to revere more and more, with unfortunate results, as will be shown below. Finally, deprived of their temple and land, the Jews began to develop a national identity while still in captivity. No matter where they were, their hearts began to turn to Jerusalem; and, from then on, no matter where they were, it would be so. For the rest of history they would believe above all else that they were the chosen people, and they would remain, for the most part, a people of identity.

Out of love for the law and their need to keep it and their national identity alive, the synagogue arose as an institution. Some even think that the first synagogue was in Babylon. The synagogue became the center of Jewish life. It also formed a pattern that was followed by the Christians, the Moslems, and even the Latter-day Saints. Synagogues, cathedrals, chapels, mosques and meetinghouses are centers of religious life with a common origin in the captivity of Judah.

JUDAH'S CHANCE TO REESTABLISH COVENANT

The repossession of the land and the rebuilding of the temple did not go smoothly. The initial group, though small, was able to lay the foundation of the temple without delay. But the people who had filled the vacuum that Israel and Judah had left in the surrounding areas began to realize the implications of the rebuilding of Jerusalem and especially the temple. First, they offered to help in the hope of worming their way in and taking over. When they were rebuffed, they developed a vigorous opposition which succeeded in retarding any immediate progress. Then, about 520 B.C., the prophets Haggai and Zechariah joined forces to push the work forward through rebuke and encouragement. There was still much work to do, but the opposition was growing stronger and not only threatened to stop the work but to destroy what had been accomplished. The little community of Jews lacked the leadership necessary to push the work any further.

Through this period the attention of Ezra, an expert in the holy books, and Nehemiah, an able administrator and personal advisor to the Persian king, was drawn to their plight. Both arranged to go to the Holy Land, and they performed monumental services. By properly assessing the situation and then cleverly handling available resources, Nehemiah succeeded masterfully. His first task was to repair the massive holes and breaks in the wall around Jerusalem. Working intently before the opposition could mobilize to thwart them, the Jews succeeded in repairing the walls in just fifty-two days. Once the city was secure, the population of the area was increased. In this way the hold of the Jews on the land was secured. Nehemiah and Ezra were governors over a number of years. Under Nehemiah, legislation was passed to assure a continuation of temple worship. Through the work of Ezra, attention was focused on the importance of the law. Though political freedom was withheld, the Jews were free to live the law of God. All over the Middle East the Jews turned to the holy books as never before in their history. Unfortunately, for the most part it was not to find God.

JUDAH TURNS TO LAW, NOT COVENANT

What promised to be a new dawn for the covenant fellowship between God and Israel turned out to be only an extension of the long night of darkness. Summarizing perfectly the cause of this, the prophet Jacob declared:

> But behold, the Jews were a stiffnecked people; and they despised the words of plainness, and killed the prophets, and sought for things that they could not understand. Wherefore, because of their blindness, which blindness came by looking beyond the mark, they must needs fall. . . . (Jacob 4:14.)

The mark the Jews looked beyond was Christ. In so doing, they did not come to understand that Christ, not the law, was the source of their salvation. The result was a new kind of idolatry more tenacious and insidious than the old. This one held to the form of godliness but turned its back on the very poor. Except for the spiritually alert, its seductive power was almost impossible to resist. Few tried. Even the rebukes of the prophets did not dissuade them. Instead, they rebelled and, as did their fathers, sought the lives of holy men. By 400 B.C. the voice of prophecy was stilled in all Palestine and apostasy increased. Schoolmen, philosophers, and theologians began to pull apart and analyze the doctrinal fabric of the law and the prophets. Those who became skilled in interpretation soon had followers. From these came the sects of Christ's day—doctors, lawyers, scribes, Pharisees, Sadducees, Herodians—who all vied

and competed with one another. The result was a hedging
up of the law so that no one could penetrate to its saving
core—Jesus Christ, who was Israel's Lord, Jehovah.

COVENANT TO BE FULFILLED

By the time of Christ, little remained of Judah's tie
with God. Reflecting upon this, Jesus told his disciples:
"The scribes and the Pharisees sit in Moses' seat. All
therefore whatsoever they bid you observe, that observe
and do; but do not ye after their works: for they say, and
do not." (Matthew 23:2-3.) The scribes and Pharisees
had complicated and multiplied the law, and prophetic
authority had been usurped by the intellectual elite. Yet,
so strong were the bonds of the covenants made to the
fathers that despite this low spiritual depth God had not
abandoned his people. In fulfillment of ancient promises,
God's son was born in the house of David. In fact, he was
sent at that time for the very reasons that only the Jews
would kill him. (See 2 Nephi 10:1-6.) Because he did not
meet their preconceived expectations they rejected and
killed him. From that point on they were abandoned. Once
again they were driven from their promised land—this
time for nearly two thousand years. The force of the covenant with their fathers nevertheless remained and was to
be totally fulfilled. But this was to be in the latter days.
(See Deuteronomy 4:25-30.)

Today we are seeing, as never before, the fruit of those
premortal and ancient covenants. Not because of any real
worthiness on their part, but because of his mercy, God has
begun the process of gathering all Israel home. Part of the
promised land is Judah's once more. But more important,

the covenant is restored in these last days in its fulness to the house of Ephraim, from whom it will go to all the tribes. To this covenant and through it all Israel can be gathered. But this time, the tribes will be perfectly united in righteousness and welded together in Christ. Upon them all — Asher and Ephraim, Judah and Dan, Mannasseh and Naphtali, all the tribes — shall come a fulness of the blessings of the Father. As Ezekiel exulted:

> . . . From all your idols, will I cleanse you.
>
> A new heart also will I give you, and a new spirit will I put within you: and I will take away the stony heart out of your flesh, and I will give you an heart of flesh.
>
> And I will put my spirit within you, and cause you to walk in my statutes, and ye shall keep my judgments, and do them.
>
> And ye shall dwell in the land that I gave to your fathers; and ye shall be my people, and I will be your God. (Ezekiel 36:25-28.)

4

Israel's Neighbors

On a sandy barren bluff the great Pyramids and the Sphinx stand a mute and sightless vigil over the city of Cairo. Only a few feet to the east is the incredibly beautiful narrow ribbon of green that stretches from the Mediterranean to the Aswan Dam some four hundred miles south and nourishes nearly all of Egypt's teeming millions. But here at the Pyramids there is nothing but the dry monotony of sand that has not been washed by rain for centuries.

It is almost better to see the Pyramids among the tourist's slides or on the pages of *National Geographic*. Somehow the close proximity, the shimmering heat, and the ubiquitous and persistent souvenir merchants rob these monuments to past tyranny of their glamour and grandeur. Even their size is hard to grasp up close. Somehow they don't look so big. And the beauty flees as they seem to slump into shapeless blobs of colorless stone.

Back in the tall hotel on the bank of the Nile in the sunset glow, the Pyramids create a different feeling. Now they look red, as though still stained by the blood that built them. The traveler is glad he saw them from this vantage point. Now he will have a mental image of them that retains some of the majesty he once felt when he knew them only by story and picture.

As the sunset fades and darkness reduces the great Pyramids to silhouettes on the skyline, the imagination reaches out and tries to span the centuries. By and by a different people appear on the scene, an ancient people sweating and toiling in the rigors of cruel bondage. The traveler watches as they strain and struggle under the lash of their masters. Slowly the Pyramids take form—the huge cubes of the superstructure, the long, narrow, descending and ascending passageways, the tiny tomb deep inside, and finally the beautiful facing stones long since gone. A pharaoh dies and his body is ceremoniously deposited in the tomb room of the great Pyramid. Thus the Pyramid becomes a monument to a comparatively useless life and to thousands of man-years of wasted toil.

As the vision fades and the great Pyramids again become a silhouette on the skyline, the traveler is impressed that this is not the only memorial to oppression. There on the skyline stands the great Pyramid's two lesser companions and out of view are others. Additonal kinds of monuments by the thousands are found up and down more than four hundred miles of the Nile River basin, their construction spanning nearly three thousand years of time— almost half of the earth's mortal existence! Each of these shrines to dead men, whether standing or buried, restored or crumbled, combine with the others to bear forceful if mute witness to the same tragedy—millennia of wasted human life.

Having stood on the parched sand and felt the oppressive heat of the wind and sun, the traveler does not find it hard to empathize with those whose broken bones lay under the hills of sand and stone. This becomes especially true as he realizes that with some of those he has ties both physical and spiritual. In that land are buried those who mark the beginning of his own heritage—Ephraim and Manasseh, Judah and Levi, Simeon and Naphtali, Reuben and Issachar, Dan and Gad, Zebulon and Asher, and finally Benjamin. It was their children who knew the taskmaster's whip and toiled under years of bondage. It seems ironic that the nation which God chose to set the example of freedom, peace, and holiness should grow to maturity chafed with the manacles of slavery. And yet, in another way, it seems fitting; for during its history Israel would be found far more in bondage than in freedom. There are two primary reasons for this: geography, and Israel's spiritual vacillations.

It should be kept in mind that there is a direct interplay between geography and the history of any given region. In fact, geography very often predetermines an area's historical development. Good lands and sufficient water yield abundant crops and allow time for other pursuits, good or bad. Poor lands, on the other hand, can produce poverty. In addition, mountains and deserts act as barriers. Oases, green belts, and river valleys provide means to penetrate these and thus help determine trade routes and highways. These factors combined to place the Holy Land at the very crossroads of the ancient world. It was situated at the extreme southwestern tip of a great fertile crescent which arched first north then southeast to the Persian Gulf. Its location made Palestine the land-bridge between the continents of Asia and Africa and therefore the connecting point between great rival powers. Over this land travelled the richest caravans. Over this land travelled the greatest armies. Whoever controlled the land had access to great wealth and at the same time to a kind of buffer zone which could delay the approach of hostile forces, thus buying precious time. For these reasons the area was coveted and fought over by many of the great empires. The ascendency and demise of ancient powers is reflected in the record of the overlordship of the Holy Land.

It was God who specified the location of Palestine, and he designed it to fulfill his purposes. Because of its location, it was in touch with all and touched all. This land could not be ignored; neither would its inhabitants, nor the message of its prophets.

It was not Israel's neighbors that were her major problem, however. It was her own spiritual weakness. Without this weakness she would have remained great and safe among the most powerful nations of the ancient world. The Lord had brought her out of Egypt to be a people of inheritance (see Deuteronomy 4:38). He promised her that she could subdue all her enemies. (See Deuteronomy 7:22-25.) This, however, was not without condition. As Moses eloquently explained, her task was to

> diligently keep all these commandments which I command you, to do them, to love the Lord your God, to walk in all his ways, and to cleave unto him;
> Then will the Lord drive out all these nations from before

you, and ye shall possess greater nations and mightier than yourselves.

Every place whereon the soles of your feet shall tread shall be yours: from the wilderness and Lebanon, from the river, the river Euphrates, even unto the uttermost sea shall your coast be. (Deuteronomy 11:22-24.)

Israel failed to keep the covenants, as was shown in the previous chapter. But in his mercy, the Lord did not destroy her outright but first sought to bring her to him. When more mild ways failed, he used Israel's neighbors as a scourge to humble her and to keep her in remembrance of him. Thus the Lord declared:

. . . Because that this people hath transgressed my covenant which I commanded their fathers, and have not hearkened unto my voice;

I also will not henceforth drive out any from before them of the nations which Joshua left when he died:

That through them I may prove Israel, whether they will keep the way of the Lord to walk therein, as their fathers did keep it, or not. (Judges 2:20-22.)

Though Israel was vastly outnumbered and completely surrounded by nations whose ideology and life-style were alien to their own and who openly coveted her land, she would have had nothing to fear from them if she had walked continually in God's ways. Because she did not, they were allowed to come against her as a kind of last effort on God's part to bring Israel to him. Had she fully repented at any point along the way, the Lord's aid and protection would have been restored.

Though God allowed these foreign nations to act as his scourge to keep Israel in remembrance of him, Israel was still responsible for its actions. Failure to accept him, rebellion against his prophets, and atrocities perpetrated on his people did not go unpunished. They were responsible for the use of their own agency. To fulfill his purposes, God will deliberately raise up a man or nation whom he knows will rebel against him. A case in point was the pharaoh who opposed Moses. To him the Lord said: "And in very deed for this cause have I raised thee up, for to shew in thee my power; and that my name may be declared throughout all the earth. As yet exaltest thou thyself against my people." (Exodus 9:16-17.) On this, Brigham Young and Willard Richards have written:

> To accomplish [His purposes] it was needful that He should meet with opposition to give Him an opportunity to manifest His power; therefore He raised up a man, even Pharaoh, who, He foreknew, would harden his heart against God of his own free will and choice, and would withstand the Almighty [and, thus, fulfill] the purposes of the Most High. (*HC*, 4:263.)

The same could be said of the Assyrians and Babylonians as well as of the Moabites and Philistines. Nevertheless, each in turn justly came under the judgments of God.

We will now turn our attention to those nations with whom ancient Israel had contact, that we might better appreciate not only biblical history but also the role these nations played in the service of God.

EGYPT

Though not as old as the civilizations in Mesopotamia, Egypt's history reaches back into the shadowy world where history is vague and uncertain in the minds of secular scholars. From the book of Abraham we learn that Egypt was discovered by the daughter of Ham and that she settled her sons upon it. The eldest, whose name was Pharaoh, established a form of patriarchal government by which he reigned. (See Abraham 1:21-24.) Eventually, other waves of settlers or conquerers, as well as revolts in the land, forced these people south. This apparently took place between Abraham's visit and the arrival of Joseph over 160 years later. It is well to not take any unscriptural chronology of Egypt too seriously. The pharaohs were prone to rewrite history, as the Greeks did and the Russians do, so that they could claim glory that belonged to others. No doubt this is how the records of Joseph, Moses, and others were obliterated from secular Egyptian history.

Egypt has been called the breadbasket of the ancient Middle East. The yearly flood of the Nile continually spread fertile soil over the flood plains. At the same time the Nile acted as a continuous source of water supply. All this combined to allow excellent production of grains, dates, and so forth, even when other countries were suffering from drought. That is not to say that the Egyptians were without worry. The Bible tells of an extended famine which plagued Egypt during the time when Joseph was in ascendency. For the most part, however, Egypt was able to survive these droughts with sufficient surplus to sell to other people. This could well have been the reason the Lord had the family of Israel settle there. Famine was a great and recurring difficulty faced by those living during the time of Abraham to Moses and on down through Israel's possession of the promised land. Hunger influenced the course of history a great deal at this time. By dwelling in one of the most fertile areas of Egypt, the children of Israel were able to escape the shortage of food which otherwise would have prevented them from becoming the focal point of nations which the Lord intended.

Israel's stay in Egypt had grave spiritual consequences, however. Many of the Israelites were seduced by the Egyptian religion. Through Ezekiel the Lord described their condition just before the Exodus:

> In the day that I lifted up mine hand unto them, to bring them forth of the land of Egypt. . . .
>
> . . . said I unto them, Cast ye away every man the abominations of his eyes, and defile not yourselves with the idols of Egypt: I am the Lord your God.
>
> But they rebelled against me, and would not hearken unto me: they did not every man cast away the abominations of their eyes, neither did they forsake the idols of Egypt. (Ezekiel 20:6-8.)

Indeed, the incident with the golden calf in the wilds of Sinai was nothing more than a reversion to the worship of the old Egyptian gods. For centuries Israel was not able to climb from under the shadow of idolatry.

There are a number of reasons why the idolatry of the Egyptians had such a tenacious hold on the Hebrews. Besides its appeal to the lusts of the flesh and the desires of the natural man to be in agreement with the accepted cultures, this religion was closer to the truth than most others which Israel encountered. The Book of Mormon and Pearl of Great Price show that the ancient patriarchs were far more knowledgeable about the nature of Christ and his mission than most scholars are willing to believe. (Compare, for example, Ether 3:6-16; 1 Nephi 19:10.) We know that the Hebrews had such a knowledge as they entered Egypt. Once there, instead of finding a religion totally alien to their own, they found one with striking similarities. First, there was the Egyptian belief in an afterlife, resurrection, and judgment. Second, they believed in a Christlike god, Osiris, who suffered mutilation and death, and who rose again to become king of the underworld and judge of the dead. (See Wallis Budge, *Egyptian Religion*, 2d ed. [New York: Bell Publishing Co., 1959], pages 6-7.) And finally, they believed in a rather convincing imitation of temple worship from which the Hebrews could not have been very far removed. (See Hugh Nibley, *The Message of the Joseph Smith Papyri: An Egyptian Endowment* [Salt Lake City: Deseret Book Co., 1975], page xiii.) The basis of this similarity went back, very likely, to the first pharaoh, who sought to copy the endowment and the patriarchal order. (See Abraham 1:26-7.)

All of these factors must have served to draw into the Egyptian camps those Israelites who were rebellious or weak in the faith. Eventually, the pure religion of Jacob became adulterated. It retained some elements of true worship, but these were intermingled with the philosophies of the Egyptians. Though there is no record to support this in the Bible, perhaps it was because of apostasy that God allowed the Hebrews to go into slavery. Whatever the case, history does provide some interesting information about Egypt during this period.

Not too long before Joseph arrived there, Egypt had been invaded and taken over by the Hyksos, a Semitic people from the north. Possibly these people would have been favorably disposed toward other promising Semites, such as Joseph and his brothers, and would have treated them kindly. Eventually, the native Egyptians revolted and were successful in driving out the conquerers, which brought in the era known in Egyptian history as the "New Kingdom." During it the throne was occupied by some of the most powerful pharaohs Egypt ever knew. It is not surprising that some of these would be suspicious of and unfriendly toward the Hebrews. The rapid growth of the

Israelite population and their mounting influence caused the Egyptians to be jealous and to fear that the Hebrews might attempt to overthrow the Egyptian rulers. As a consequence, the Israelites were forced into servitude and efforts were made to halt or reduce their number by murdering their infants. Finally, the Lord called Moses to break the chains of bondage by a marvelous display of heaven-sent miracles and power.

Prior to the Exodus the Egyptians had taken a strong interest in Palestine and had extended their influence over it, hoping to prevent any recurring foreign domination. But the Egyptians never physically occupied the area. Rather, they stationed troops in a few key locations, primarily to keep the trade routes open, to act as a check on hostile nomads, make sure that their tributaries paid taxes and formed no alliances against Egypt.

During most of the time of the Israelite occupation of Palestine, Egypt continued to be the great world power and continued to think of Palestine as a part of her sphere of influence. During the mid-thirteenth century B.C., however, Egypt was threatened by the invasion-migration of the Sea People of whom the Philistines were a part. This problem in addition to her internal difficulties kept the Egyptian influence in Palestine very weak. By 1150 B.C. Egypt lost the area totally and was replaced by the Philistines, who held the coastal region, and the Hebrews, who for the most part occupied the hill country.

The Egyptians did not appear again in Palestine until the reign of David, when, taking advantage of his war with the Syrians, they captured Gezer. But they were not in a position to hold it; and, probably in a face-saving gesture, they gave it as a dowry to a royal Egyptian bride of Solomon. This friendly relationship between the countries did not outlive Solomon.

By 950 B.C. the Lybians had succeeded in conquering Egypt. One of the Lybian pharaohs, Shishak, gave refuge to Jeroboam when Solomon ordered his execution. Shortly after Jeroboam returned and set up the kingdom of Israel, Shishak attacked Judah and then Israel. His campaigns were successful in reducing the power of the two Israelite kingdoms and in amassing vast plunder. After this show of force, the Egyptians were content to leave the area alone for some time.

Palestine was not left free, however. Assyria was able to put Palestine under its control by 770 B.C. In 724 B.C. the Northern Kingdom revolted. Hoshea, then king, called upon Pharaoh So for assistance. The Egyptian help was inadequate and halfhearted. The ten tribes were devastated and taken away into captivity. The Assyrians then moved not only against Judah but against Egypt as well, placing both under its domination. But by the early seventh century B.C. Egypt regained her independence and began a program of resurgence. She accomplished this through the use of mercenaries, many of whom were Jews.

In the meantime, Babylonia and her northern allies conquered Assyria, and Babylonia began to be the new world power. Egypt, under Pharaoh Necho, felt threatened and launched an army through Israel to stop the Babylonian advance. Josiah, king of Judah, attempted to block this intrusion into his domain. He was unsuccessful and was killed during the battle at Megiddo in 609 B.C. This served to delay the encounter between the Egyptians and Babylonians for four years. A decisive battle was eventually fought at Carchemish. The Egyptians were forced back to their own lands and Palestine fell to the Babylonians.

The Egyptians were still anxious, however, to reduce the power of Babylon over an area so close to home. Pharaoh Apries conspired with Zedekiah, king of Judah, in an attempt to throw off Babylonian domination. This rebellion failed, resulting in the sack of Jerusalem and the deportation of most of Judah's inhabitants. Thereafter, Egypt lost any significant influence over the area. But Egypt became the homeland of many Jews who fled from the Babylonians, having for over fifteen hundred years a significant Jewish population. In the fourth century B.C. Egypt was conquered by Alexander the Great. After his death it fell into the hands of Ptolemy, one of his generals. Egypt was ruled by the family of Ptolemy until conquered by the Romans in the days of Julius Caesar and Mark Anthony. Cleopatra was the last of this ruling Greek family.

TRANSJORDAN

When Moses led Israel away from Egypt toward the Holy Land, he moved her through areas already populated. These were, respectively, Edom, Moab, and Ammon. Most of the people inhabiting these areas were related to Israel. The Edomites were descendants of Esau, the elder brother of Jacob. The Ammonites and Moabites were the descendants of Abraham's nephew, Lot, through his daughters.

The boundaries between these small nations were continually in a state of flux due to temporary ascendancies of one local nation or another or of world powers. The geographical location of each can be generally established, however. Edom, sometimes referred to as Mt. Seir, was located south of the Dead Sea. It stretched from the Gulf of Aqaba to the River Zered. Bordering on the Arabian Desert, the land is generally hot and dry. Its mountains did afford forage for sheep and cattle as well as protection for the people. Moab bordered Edom and stretched north nearly the full length of the Dead Sea to the River Arnon and very often beyond. It was slightly more fertile than its southern neighbor, providing good pasture for sheep and cattle from which most of the population obtained a livelihood. Ammon initially bordered Moab on the north and encompassed the area between the Arnon and Jabbok rivers. Early in its history part of this land was taken from it by the Amorites and it was confined to an area east of the Jabbok. The Amorites were Canaanites whose territory included most of the hill country on both sides of the Jordan. The area of the Ammonites and Amorites is still more fertile than that of the south. Through irrigation practices most of the population was able to sustain itself by farming — grain crops and olive orchards predominating. But this was augmented by grazing, especially to the east where water became increasingly scarce.

The entire area, from Edom to Ammon, bordering as it did on the western fringe of the Arabian Desert, was continually vulnerable to encroachments and raids from fierce desert nomads. This gave rise to strong central governments which could organize and supply troops as well as build fortifications. Though each developed its own peculiarities, they all became monarchies. Almost from their inception, these small kingdoms warred against one another, trying to put the others into vassalage, but there was never

enough power in any one of them to completely subdue and
unite the area. As a consequence, there was a continual shift
in power and territorial lines.

The Amorites existed as a people long before the other
Transjordan kingdoms. Their initial area of influence was
generally confined to the hill country of Palestine. Abraham formed an alliance with the Amorites at Hebron and,
with their aid, routed the four kings who had attacked the
cities of the plains. They had taken Lot and his family
captive in the process and Abraham rescued him. About
four hundred years later, when the Israelites began their
conquest of Palestine, the Amorite kings, Sihon of Heshbon
and Og of Bashan, controlled most of the northern Transjordan. The Israelite victory over these two kings was the
first step in the invasion of the promised land. After the land
was settled, these people became menials and were eventually absorbed into the Israelite nation.

The next oldest kingdom was Edom, where there were
kings "before there reigned any king over the children of
Israel" (Genesis 36:31). Esau had already occupied that
land before Jacob returned from Haran. His descendants
were able to subdue the original occupants, the Norites, and
eventually incorporate them into their numbers. At the time
of the Exodus, Israel asked permission to cross this land via
the Kings Highway, a major road crossing the Jordanian
highlands. This request was refused. But God would not let
Israel come against them at the time because of their blood
relationship. After Israel was established in the promised
land Joshua allotted the territory of Judah up to the borders
of Edom but refused to let them encroach on Edomite lands.
The Edomites did, on occasion, raid the territory of Judah.
Eventually Saul waged war against them, and David was

successful in subduing the area. This allowed Solomon to exploit their copper mines and to build a port at Ezion-Geber. When Israel became fractured, Edom was successful in gaining her independence. Thereafter, she was not beyond raiding and plundering Judah until she was incorporated into the Assyrian-Babylonian empire. When Judah fell to Nebuchadnezzar the Edomites rejoiced. For this manifestation of bitter hatred the prophets foretold of judgments upon her. (See Jeremiah 44:7-12; Ezekiel 25:12-14; Joel 3:19; Amos 9:12.) In the fifth century B.C. she fell to the Arabs, and in the third century B.C. she was overrun by the Nabataeans, never to rise again.

There were settled villages in Moab in the time of Abraham. Lot's posterity, through his eldest daughter, eventually became the dominant power. Just before the exodus, the Amorite king Sihon was successful in wresting part of the northern territory away from Moab. When Israel came upon the scene, Moab, like Edom, refused to let her travel via the Kings Highway. Again God would not allow Israel to attack her. Instead, Israel circumnavigated these two lands and moved toward Canaan through the territory of King Sihon. Israel's successful conquest of this area caused Balak, the king of Moab, to fear she might attack him from this northern vantage point. He sought help from the prophet Balaam. Under the inspiration of God, however, Balaam was unable to curse Israel as Balak wanted. Instead, he ended up blessing Israel and cursing Moab.

During the time of the Judges, Moab held the Israelite territory around Jericho. David was later able to subdue this land, but shortly after the time of Solomon it broke away. Under Omri, king of Israel, it was temporarily recaptured, but after this it remained free until subdued by the Assyrians and Babylonians. It finally ceased to have an independent existence when it was overrun by the Arabs in the third century B.C. Because of its continual hostility toward Israel, the prophets often mentioned that divine punishment would come against it. (See Isaiah 15, 16, 25; Jeremiah 9:26; Ezekiel 25:8-11; Amos 2:1-3.)

The kingdom of Ammon was settled by the son of Lot who was born to his youngest daughter. His descendants overcame the natives and established an effective government. During the Exodus the Ammonites joined with their kinsmen the Moabites in hiring Balaam to curse Israel. During the time of the Judges, Ammon captured Israelite lands east of Jordan and subjected the area of Gilead. When the Ammonites moved against the city of Jabesh-Gilead, King Saul united the Israelite tribes and drove off the Ammonites. During the first years of David's reign the two nations were on friendly terms; but, when a new king abused a peaceful diplomatic mission sent by David, war broke out. David's generals were able to subdue the area. Some Ammonites befriended Israel and willingly served in her armies. A number of Solomon's wives were from this nation. During the time of the divided kingdom, Ammon joined Moab and Edom in harassing Israel. After the fall of Jerusalem, their king provoked further trouble with the remaining Jews, causing many to flee to Egypt. Because of the Ammonites' continual molestations, they, too, came under the censure of the prophets. (See Jeremiah 49:1-6; Ezekiel 21:20; 25:1-7; Amos 1:13-15.) As a nation, they lasted longer than Edom and Moab, finally losing their identity in the first century B.C.

CANAANITES

Technically the Canaanites were not Israel's neighbors, since it was on land formerly possessed by them that Israel settled. Their culture did influence Israel, however, and until at least the time of Solomon there were a number of Canaanite strongholds scattered throughout the land. The early Canaanite domain included all of Palestine and much of Syria. The inhabitants of the land were not homogeneous. Nor was there a centralized government over the whole before Israel invaded the area. The predominant group was the Amorites, and this name was sometimes applied to the inhabitants of the whole region. Successive waves of people moving into and through the lands caused a continual change in the ethnic composition of the population and interfered with consolidation. A number of cities, each presided over by a king, became strong enough to control the area around them. Their borders were fluid, however, each king vying with his neighbors for a greater area of control. As noted earlier, Egypt had considerable control over the area, extracted tribute from it, and encouraged the disunity that prevailed. Not being able to present a unified front, the populace suffered from the continual domination of the larger powers. In addition, the growth of the Transjordan kingdoms as well as invasions by the Sea People from the north and west and the Aramaeans from the east caused continual ethnic and political changes. Only the conquest of the land by the Hebrews brought a season of stability. By about 1200 B.C. the Canaanites had been effectively integrated into the various peoples who controlled the emerging nations and so ceased to be a distinct people.

Long after the Canaanites disappeared as an entity, their religion continued to affect the land. Their chief deity was the Ugaritic nature-god, Baal. Even before entering the promised land Israel was seduced to its worship when the women of Moab introduced it at Balaam's encouragement. (See Numbers 31:16; Revelation 2:14.) The worship of this god had double appeal. The first was to the natural man; for Baal worship included sexual orgies and perversions. The second was tied to the climatic conditions which prevailed over the whole area. The land was totally dependent upon adequate rainfall for both crops and pasture land. When the rains came on time and in abundance there was prosperity. When they did not, all suffered. Therefore, Baal, as god of the weather, was continually appealed to. Israel was affected by this mentality, the result being a continual conflict between the worship of Jehovah and the worship of Baal or natural law. This conflict finally reached a head when Elijah sealed the heavens so that it would not rain for three years and then challenged the priests of Baal to a contest. The purpose of this was to decide once and for all who supplied the rain—Jehovah or Baal. It is one of the tragedies of Israel's history that Jehovah's spectacular victory did not have lasting results. At the same time we can see why the stiff-necked Israelites would take the easy way out. Rather than faithfully keeping the covenants, they put their hopes in the permissive Baal. The tragic results of their folly were discussed in chapter 3.

PHILISTINES

In the early part of the twelfth century B.C. Egypt and many Canaanite coastal towns were invaded by a large force known as the Sea People. Their homeland was the Aegean island system over which Crete was the principle power. Some believe that the Philistines were part of this group. They settled over the southwestern coastal plain of Palestine with little or no resistance from the natives. The art of warfare was cultivated by them and they were able to maintain very effective armies. As they expanded into the hill country to the south and west, they ran into the Israelites who also were subduing the area. There was a continual clash between these two nations. Until the time of David, the Philistines had a central government composed of each of the leaders from its five principle cities: Gaza, Ashkelon, Ashdod, Ekron, and Gath. These men acted in a council which could overrule any individual leader. Their principal deity was the fish-god, Dagon; but they also joined in the worship of Baal and other local divinities.

During the reign of the Judges, the Philistines kept continual pressure upon Israel and were able to capture and destroy a number of principal towns including Shiloh, from which they carried the ark of the covenant. This sacrilege brought a plague upon them and they sent the ark back. Saul was successful for a while in pushing the Philistines back into their coastal area, but they succeeded in defeating Saul at Gilboa and reestablishing some control over that area. After David was anointed king, he waged war against them. He was successful in subduing Gath and imposing vassalage upon it. The other cities supplied him with mercenary troops.

From this point on, the Philistines ceased to have a centralized government and their history is that of the individual cities. It is speculated that the reason for this was that the continual warring virtually wiped out the strong

military class, allowing the more peaceful Philistine-
Canaanites to take over. Toward the end of the united
kingdom, and for a long time after its division, the Philistines were under the control of Egypt. It was from Philistia
that Pharaoh Shishak launched his attack against the Israelites. Over the next fifty years there was continual warfare
between Israel and Philistia, with neither side able to win a
decisive victory. Eventually the area fell under the control of
Assyria. Several revolts brought recapture. Finally,
Nebuchadnezzar extinguished any hope of Philistine independence.

BABYLONIANS AND ASSYRIANS

The fertile and lush area between the Tigris and
Euphrates rivers attracted a number of the descendants of
Noah. Two cities gained strength very early: Ur of the
Chaldees and Babylon. According to the Bible, Babylon was
originally founded by Nimrod, a grandson of Ham (Genesis
10:6-9). Ancient tradition suggests that he set up a government there in opposition to and in imitation of the patriarchal government established by God through Noah.
Nimrod is credited with the introduction of idolatry among
the children of men. (See Hugh Nibley, *Lehi in the Desert and
The World of the Jaredites* [Salt Lake City: Bookcraft, 1952],
pages 154-57.) It was under his direction that the Tower of
Babel was built as a pseudo-temple. The Lord scattered the
people and confounded their language to put an end to
this mischief. (Nimrod's goal was a dictatorship over the
earth's inhabitants.) For a time Babylon appears to have
remained empty.

In the meantime, Ur, in the land of the Chaldees, just above the Persian Gulf, came into prominence. It gradually extended its influence over a broad area. Severe famines brought an end to the kingdom, however. Its rulers were replaced by invaders from Elam and seminomads from the west desert. It is from this era that the migrations of Terah and Abraham began.

Meanwhile, Babylon was reestablished and began its climb to power. Under Hammurabi, it defeated all opposition and ruled from the Persian Gulf to Mari, an ancient town in the north near the present border of Iraq and Syria. About 1595 B.C., however, it was attacked from the north by the Hittites. Shortly thereafter the Kassites were successful in winning much of the territory. In the centuries which followed, Babylon was generally free but quite weak. Continual raids from peoples from the north pulled Babylonian pressure off Palestine and allowed the Israelites time to establish themselves in the land.

All this time another city had been growing. This was Nineveh, founded by Asshur, a son of Shem, at the time Nimrod was ruling in Babylon. (Sometimes the prophets referred to Assyria as Asshur.) As with Babylon, it suffered a few setbacks due to invasions but was able to overcome these. In 890 B.C. Nineveh began to take vigorous military action against its oppressors. By 860 B.C. it had subdued all the upper Euphrates and reached west as far as Lebanon and the Mediterranean Sea. This marked the beginning of the sustained pressure which would eventually bring Assyria into conflict with Israel.

During the time Assyria was expanding into Babylonia and establishing control in the upper Mediterranean area, an already divided Israel was being warned to repent lest this savage foreign power destroy them. The prophets Joel, Hosea, Jonah, Amos and Isaiah issued these warnings. In 732 the Assyrian King Prel took Syria and marched down the coast as far as Gaza exacting tribute. When the kingdom of Israel, after listening to overtures from Egypt, refused to pay tribute a few years later, Shalmaneser II, son and successor of Prel, laid seige to Samaria, destroyed it, and took the ten tribes to the north where they disappeared from history.

For the next few years Assyria was faced with a series of internal revolts. The Babylonians made a bid for freedom and went so far as to ask Hezekiah, king of Judah, for help. Isaiah's warning that such an alliance would be disastrous proved to be correct. Assyria sacked Babylon, suppressed the revolts, and under Sennacherib moved against Judea. The kingdom was saved only through divine intervention. Hezekiah humbled himself before the Lord and pleaded for help. Word came from Isaiah that his prayer was heard. That night a plague, or some other disaster, decimated the Assyrian army, forcing Sennacherib to withdraw. But within a few years Assyria was back and effectively put all of Palestine under its control and marched into Egypt.

Assyria tried to compel all she conquered to worship Asher, her chief deity. Almost immediately revolts broke out. Ashurbanipal was successful in putting these down for the most part and in expanding the kingdom to its greatest extent. This effort put great strain on the empire, however. When Assyria pulled its troops from the frontier to suppress a Babylonian revolt, a number of areas, including Egypt and Palestine, were successful in throwing off the Assyrian yoke. At this same time bands of Scythians from the area of the Black Sea invaded the upper Euphrates. The combined armies of the Babylonians and Scythians were successful in sacking Nineveh and conquering the whole area.

Babylon wasted no time in securing a treaty with the Scythians and in consolidating its gains. Egypt, in the meantime, was staking claim to Palestine and Syria. The new Babylonian king, Nebuchadnezzar, launched three campaigns to drive Egypt out. The final battle took place at Carchemish, where the Egyptian army was routed. This opened the way for complete Babylonian domination in Syria, Palestine, and the Transjordan area. As pointed out earlier, however, Egypt continued to be a viable force. She was, in fact, the only nation that had a chance of stopping the Babylonian onslaught. The courts of Egypt and those of the nations who hoped for her help became boiling pots of intrigue. But at no time, even when combined with other nations, was Egypt able to make any headway against the Babylonian power.

About 604 B.C. Nebuchadnezzar moved his army through Palestine, strengthening his garrisons, securing the frontier, collecting tribute, and gathering hostages. Daniel, along with other children of the Jewish elite, was taken to Babylon at this time. (Chronologists place this captivity all the way from 608 B.C. to 602 B.C.) In 601 B.C. Babylon fought what proved to be her final major battle with Egypt. Both sides sustained heavy loss, and Babylon withdrew to resupply. It was at this time that Jehoiakim, king of Judah, rejected the counsel of Jeremiah and transferred his loyalty to Egypt, a move which proved foolhardy. Three years later Babylon was back in force and attacked Jerusalem. After a long seige the city fell and Jehoiakim was replaced by Zedekiah. They were both vassals of Nebuchadnezzar. At this point a number of prophets appeared on the scene declaring that wickedness had brought the disaster and warning that the worst was yet to come unless there was swift obedience. One of these prophets was that same Lehi who, under God's direction, eventually left the city to establish his posterity in America.

Zedekiah, encouraged by Egypt, rebelled. This brought the full wrath of Babylon upon Judea. Jerusalem was destroyed in 587 B.C. and many Jews were taken into captivity at that time. A final deportation took place six years later, leaving only a scattered few of the poorest Jews in the area. They were unable to hinder the Transjordanian kingdoms from grabbing various areas. The Babylonians were not concerned about this takeover because these kingdoms were already under Babylonian control. From about 560 B.C. to 540 B.C. Babylon was plagued by internal problems. Various men coveted the throne; murder and intrigue weakened the power of the monarchy; unfair reforms caused the masses to revolt. Finally in 544 B.C. Nabonidus was successful in bringing order again. By this time, however, the country was weak and divided.

To the east of Babylon, Cyrus, the Persian, had been able to unite Media and Elam to his kingdom. The weakened condition of Babylon invited invasion from this growing empire. Babylon fell to Cyrus's forces in 539 B.C. and Nabonidus and Belshazzar his son were killed. The Persians were just and favorable to the Jews. Cyrus encouraged them to return to their homeland. Many, though by no means most, took the opportunity. Cyrus placed his son Cambysses on the throne as co-regent. He became king when his father fell in battle. Cambysses's death a few years later brought insurgence, and pretenders seized the throne. In 522 B.C. Darius I was successful in restoring law and order. He allowed the Jews, under Zerubbabel, to rebuild the temple at Jerusalem.

Until its capture by Alexander the Great in 331 B.C., Babylon continued to be ruled by Persian kings. The Jews, for the most part, fared well during this time. The book of Esther tells of an incident when Haman, a high official in the court of Artaxerxes, plotted to have all the Jews in the empire killed. Artaxerxes is called Ahasuerus in the King James Bible. He ruled from 465 to 425 B.C. His queen, the Jewess Esther, was able to disclose this plot and save her people. Except for this and a few local incidents, there were few serious problems for the Jews. Many, such as Daniel, Mordecai, and Esther, were placed in high state positions. Another of these was Nehemiah, who was sent to Jerusalem as governor and was successful in rebuilding and fortifying its walls. The Jews had no real allegiance to the kingdom, however. When it fell to the Macedonian army under Alexander, the Jews merely shifted their allegiance.

When Alexander died, his vast empire fell into the hands of his generals, who continually warred with each other for control. Two Greek families, the Ptolemies of Egypt and the family of Antiochus the Great of Syria, fought a great deal over Palestine. First the Ptolemies ruled this area and then the Syrian kings took over. In the third century B.C. the Syrians persecuted the Jews so badly, heaping insults on their religion and forcing them to commit idolatrous and repugnant acts, that a family filled with heroes—the Maccabees—started a revolt. Under them, both before and after the Roman dominance, the

Jews enjoyed some autonomy. Later, the Romans installed the Herodian kings, who were generally infamous in the eyes of the Jews. Throughout this interim period—between the Old and New Testament times—the Maccabean period, which lasted about a century, was perhaps the brightest spot. Many names and heroes come out of that time—men like Judas Maccabeus and Simon the Just, a great high priest. But generally speaking the whole period from Malachi to Jesus was a time of partial apostasy. The people were not bad enough to totally lose the priesthood, nor the divine intervention of God, which occurred on occasion. But apparently they never had what history has accepted as a true prophet or what most Christians and Jews have accepted as true scripture.

A NATION IN EXILE

The Old Testament ends with the Jews still under the rule of the Persians. As has been noted, the land later fell to the Macedonians. Still later it was conquered by the Romans. Each of these countries had its way with the Hebrews. The end result was what is called, in profane history, the Diaspora—the great dispersion. The house of Israel ultimately was scattered to the four corners of the world. There were a few feeble attempts to gather; but these, for the most part, were in vain. They were to remain scattered until the dispensation of the fulness of times. Instead of becoming the mighty nation and world leader that God had made possible, Israel became a nation in exile. Wickedness, rebellion and apostasy had left her powerless even to repent.

That the Lord raised up nations as scourges was an act of caring. Nothing else remained than to let Israel suffer the consequences of her folly. The brutal Assyrian onslaught left thousands dead, while the Babylonian siege of Jerusalem reduced some of that city to cannibalism. None of this was pleasing to God. Instead, he desired Israel to be as leaven through which these other nations would be brought to him. Since she would not, God used the other nations against her and began to prepare for another time and another people when his will would be done.

None of the above is meant to imply that the Lord did not know the end from the beginning. He did. The prophecies of Moses and others show this. Nevertheless, he labored with Israel in such a way that they were left without excuse. And, as a by-product that has been priceless to countless millions, the Bible was created. It is one of the greatest marvels of the world and is a handbook in law and behavior to all who have the wisdom to go to it for counsel.

5

The Rites and Practices of the Law of Moses

High upon a pinnacle of the temple, the white-robed priest gazed first at the early morning skyline above the Mount of Olives and then southward toward Hebron, the ancient burial place of Abraham. He could watch the Judean hills, well above even the palaces of Jerusalem, trade their blanket of blackness for a patchwork of grays touched ever so lightly with rose. Above his head most of the stars had yielded to the morning light which moved slowly toward the house of the Lord. Below him, his fellow priests worked to make all ready for his signal. Nothing was to be overlooked or left undone. The three fires in the great altar burned intensely, spreading a glow which played against the remaining darkness within the inner court.

Sensing that the time was right, the priest called down to those below, "The morning shineth already," to which came back the query, "Is the sky lit up as far as Hebron?" With the affirmative response, the lamb was ordered to be brought into the court. For four days it had been kept in readiness for this occasion. After letting it drink out of a golden bowl, the priests examined it once more, this time by torchlight, to reconfirm its sacrificial fitness according to Levitical law. Then the lamb was securely tied to the north side of the altar. The priest conducting the sacrifice stood on the east side and turned the animal's face to the west. At this moment the command was given to open the temple gates. As soon as the last gate was fully opened, the assigned priests blew three blasts on their silver trumpets. In this way the Levites were summoned to their duties and the city was informed that the morning sacrifice was about to be offered.

While the sun was still below the horizon, though the whole countryside was lightened by dawn, the lamb was killed. Its blood was caught in a bowl dedicated for that purpose and then sprinkled by the priest first on the northeast corner of the altar and then on the southwest corner in such a way as to cover two sides at once. The rest of the blood was poured out at the base of the altar. After this the animal was carefully prepared and certain parts were burned as the law dictated.

Every morning, including the Sabbath, when the temple was functioning under Israelite control, this ceremony was repeated. It was done again, with slight variance, in the evening. During the hours in between, other sacrifices were offered.

What was the purpose and meaning of all this carefully prescribed ritualism? The answer to this question is not as clearly given in the Old Testament as in the Book of Mormon, and the Jews know less about it than knowledgeable Latter-day Saints. The Jews, of course, have kept alive the detail and history of these sacrifices even though, except for small sects that number very few people, they no longer practice them.

SACRIFICE FORESHADOWS AND SYMBOLIZES CHRIST

Every detail of the rites and ceremonies of the religious side of the law of Moses was designed to teach the people of the coming and mission of Jesus. Nephi put it this way:

> Behold, my soul delighteth in proving unto my people the truth of the coming of Christ; for, for this end hath the law of Moses been given; and all things which have been given of God from the beginning of the world, unto man, are the typifying of him. (2 Nephi 11:4.)

The law of performances and ordinances, coupled with the specified high days, was, therefore, as a part of the law of Moses, a type or a shadow of the ministry and mission of the great Lamb of God who was to come as a sacrifice for all mankind. Thus, the ordinances of the Old Testament were not designed as mere outward observances. They were not just a kind of "work-righteousness," as Edersheim calls it (Alfred Edersheim, *The Temple: Its Ministry and Services* [Grand Rapids, Mi.: Wm. B. Eerdmans Publishing Co., 1976], page 105.) The Israelites and their priests were not justified or made holy by the mere fact of compliance with the law of Moses. "For it is not possible that the blood of bulls and of goats should take away sins" (Hebrews 10:4). Rather, these ordinances were to reveal the Christ. Speaking of sacrifices in particular, but actually revealing the purpose of all ordinances, Edersheim has stated:

The sacrifices of the Old Testament were symbolical and typical. An outward observance without any real inward meaning is only a ceremony. But a rite which has a present spiritual meaning is a symbol; and if, besides, it also points to a future reality, conveying at the same time, by anticipation, the blessing that is yet to appear, it is a type. Thus the Old Testament sacrifices were not only symbols, nor yet merely predictions by fact (as prophecy is a prediction by word), but they already conveyed to the believing Israelite the blessing that was to flow from the future reality to which they pointed. (*The Temple*, page 106.)

The prophet Abinadi put it this way: "Therefore, if ye teach the law of Moses, also teach that it is a shadow of those things which are to come—Teach them that redemption cometh through Christ the Lord. . . ." (Mosiah 16:14-15.)

Being a type and a shadow of things to come, the essential nature of the law of performances and ordinances is prophetic. It was this power which caused it to be venerated by the faithful.

Yea, and they did keep the law of Moses. . . . But notwithstanding the law of Moses, they did look forward to the coming of Christ, considering that the law of Moses was a type of his coming. . . .

Now they did not suppose that salvation came by the law of Moses; but the law of Moses did serve to strengthen their faith in Christ; and thus they did retain a hope through faith, unto eternal salvation, relying upon the spirit of prophecy, which spake of those things to come. (Alma 25:15-16.)

The purpose of this chapter is to investigate the "spirit of prophecy" which undergirded, overspread, and gave meaning to both the Mosaic sacrifices and festivals. Each major sacrifice will be explained briefly, and then its function as a revelation of the mission of the Lord will be examined. After this, each of the major festivals will be considered in the same way. But first, a few points about sacrifices in general.

SACRIFICE, AN ORDINANCE OF HOLY PRIESTHOOD

The law of sacrifice is not exclusive to the Mosaic code. The importance and mode of this law actually reaches back prior to the foundation of the world when "a preparatory redemption . . . in and through the atonement of the Only Begotten Son, who was prepared." (Alma 13:3-5.) In the premortal councils, the "Son of Man" (Moses 6:57) was chosen and prepared to be Jesus, the Christ. Thus, he was "the Lamb [who was] slain from the foundation of the world." (Moses 7:47.)

The importance of this ordinance in preparing men for the redemption is seen by the fact that the law of sacrifice, coupled with that of obedience, was the first commandment given to Adam after the Fall. Its significance was revealed as an angel proclaimed: "This thing is a similitude of the sacrifice of the Only Begotten of the Father, which is full of grace and truth. Wherefore [i.e., because the Savior, being full of grace and truth, will make the necessary sacrifice for mankind to overcome their fallen state], thou shalt do all that thou doest in the name of the Son . . . forevermore." (Moses 5:7-8.) Thus, sacrifice was the first ordinance of all ordinances designed to teach man the need to repent and come to God through the blood of Christ. Joseph Smith taught:

> That the offering of sacrifice was only to point the mind forward to Christ, we infer from these remarkable words of Jesus to the Jews: "Your Father Abraham rejoiced to see

my day: and he saw it, and was glad'' (John viii:56). So, then, because the ancients offered sacrifice it did not hinder their hearing the Gospel; but served, as we said before, to open their eyes, and enable them to look forward to the time of the coming of the Savior, and rejoice in His redemption. (*TPJS*, page 60.)

As one begins a study of the law of sacrifice he should keep in mind that the scriptures do not tell us how the ordinance was performed before the days of Moses. Doubtless, it was much more simple than the elaborate ceremony revealed at Sinai. Special laws and ordinances were given to the Israelites in Moses' day because they were a spiritually immature people. As the Book of Mormon states:

> It was expedient that there should be a law given to the children of Israel, yea, even a very strict law; for they were a stiffnecked people, quick to do iniquity, and slow to remember the Lord their God; Therefore there was a law given them, yea, a law of performances and of ordinances, a law which they were to observe strictly from day to day, to keep them in remembrance of God and their duty towards him. But behold, I say unto you, that all these things were types of things to come. (Mosiah 13:29-31.)

Because these ''types of things to come'' were revealed for a spiritually weak Israel, those living today inherit an added blessing. Through the details of the elaborate symbol system revealed to Moses, the ''spirit of prophecy'' can easily be traced and much detailed meaning about the atonement of Christ can be learned.

In addition to the fact that the sacrifices of the law of Moses were revealed to develop faith in Christ, they also were designed to assist one in overcoming the ''natural man'' and thereby becoming a Saint. In other words, through active and faithful participation in these ordinances, one ceased to be an enemy of God (alien) and became a son (citizen). (See Mosiah 3:19; 27:25-26; Ephesians 2:11-17.) President David O. McKay explained that this was a process of overcoming selfishness:

> How significant is that passage, then, which says, "By grace are ye saved through faith; and that not of yourselves; it is the gift of God." [Ephesians 2:8-10]
>
> The Lord revealed to man the Gospel, and one of the very first commandments given superseded in essence the *self-preservation* law. *It was the law of sacrifice.* The effect of this was that the best the earth produced, the best specimen in the flock or herd should not be used for self, but for God. It was God, not the earth, whom man should worship. How this simple test of sacrifice affected the divine nature as well as the carnal in man, the story of Cain and Abel graphically and appropriately illustrates. For one, the best, the "firstlings of the flock" was all too poor as a means of expressing his love and appreciation of the revelation of life that God had given; for the other, he would go through the form because God had commanded, but he would keep the best for himself.
>
> And so through the ages, this eternal conflict between the divine life of service and the earth life of carnal and sensual and selfish indulgence and ease continued. Millions lived and died believing that the whole purpose of life is to *get* and possess what earth has to give, never comprehending that the whole purpose of life is to *give*.
>
> Then in the Meridian of Time came the Saviour of man, toward whose coming man in the morning of life had looked forward, and upon whose life man in the evening of life should look in retrospect. In the meridian of the earth's history came the Son of Man declaring the eternal truth so opposed to the promises of the earth, that *he that would save his life must lose it.* ("The Atonement," *Instructor* [March 1959]: 65-66.)

MOSAIC SACRIFICIAL SYSTEM

Under the law of Moses five basic sacrifices were required: the burnt offering, the meat (or, to update the language, the food or cereal) offering, the peace offering, the sin offering, and the trespass offering. The first three constituted what were called the "sweet savor" and "voluntary" offerings. The last two were classified as "sin" and "obligatory" offerings.

Whether the sacrifices were "sweet savor" or "sin" offerings there were certain common elements. First, God determined what was to be offered and how:

> The general requisites of all sacrifices were—that they should be brought of such things, in such place and manner, and through such mediatorial agency, as God had appointed. (*The Temple,* page 109.)

Second, that which was offered had to be one's own property:

> The principle seems rather to have been that of property (*cf.* 2 Sa. xxiv. 24), the wild animals being regarded as in some sense already God's (Ps. 1. 9 ff.; *cf.* Is. xl. 16), while the domestic animals had become man's by his labours (Gn. xxii. 13 is only apparently an exception), and were in a kind of 'biotic rapport' with him. This was even more clearly the case with the nonblood offerings, which had been produced by 'the sweat of his brow' (cereals, flour, oil, wine, *etc.*), and were also staple articles of the kitchen. Property unlawfully acquired was not acceptable. (*New Bible Dictionary,* pages 115-16.)

Third, the offering was to be the best of its kind because, as a type of Jesus, its physical perfection was taken as symbolic of Jesus' mortal perfection:

> The leading features of the symbolical and typical meaning of the sacrifices are in their general outline the following.

> Every animal offered in sacrifice was to be . . . free from faults; not merely on the ground that only a faultless and perfect gift could be an offering fit for the Holy and Perfect One, but chiefly because moral faults were reflected in those of the body, and to prefigure the sinlessness and holiness of the true sacrifice, and warn the offerer that the sanctification of all his members was indispensable to a self-surrender to God, the Holy One, and to life in fellowship with Him. (C. F. Keil and F. Delitzsch, *Commentary on the Old Testament*, 25 vols. [Grand Rapids, Mi.: Wm. B. Eerdmans Publishing Co., 1978], 1:279.)

Fourth, at least a portion of each offering was totally consumed by fire:

> Fire, from its inherent power to annihilate what is perishable, ignoble, and corrupt, is a symbol in the Scriptures, sometimes of purification, and sometimes of torment and destruction. That which has an imperishable kernel within it is purified by the fire, the perishable materials which have adhered to it or penetrated within it being burned out and destroyed, and the imperishable and nobler substance being thereby purified from all dross; whilst, on the other hand, in cases where the imperishable is completely swallowed up in the perishable, no purification ensues, but total destruction by the fire (1 Cor. iii. 12, 13). Hence fire is employed as a symbol and vehicle of the Holy Spirit (Acts ii. 3, 4), and the fire burning upon the altar was a symbolical representation of the working of the purifying Spirit of God; so that the burning of the flesh of the sacrifice upon the altar "representing the purification of the man, who had been reconciled to God, through the fire of the Holy Spirit, which consumes what is flesh, to pervade what is spirit with light and life, and thus to transmute it into the blessedness of fellowship with God." (Keil and Delitzsch, 1:280.)

The Hebrew text employs a technical expression for the burning of the sacrifice when done upon the altar. This Hebrew word conveys the idea that the smoke of the offering was to ascend to God as a pleasant odor. This was because the giving of the sacrifice represented the life of the offerer, which, it was hoped would be found acceptable by Jehovah.

Fifth, salt had to be used with every offering:

> It was often used among Oriental peoples for ratifying agreements, so that salt became the symbol of fidelity and constancy. In the levitical cereal offerings (Lv. ii. 13) salt was used as a preservative to typify the eternal nature of the 'covenant of salt' existing between God and Israel (Nu. xviii. 19; 2 Ch. xiii. 5). (*New Bible Dictionary*, page 1125.)

And finally, with the exception of the cereal offering —which was never offered alone but always in company with an animal sacrifice—blood was shed. Blood is the very essence of life (Leviticus 17:10-11, 14). As such it symbolized the life which the Lord would give that men might live. Israel was forbidden not only the eating of blood but also the letting of their own blood for sacrificial purposes. Though other cultures did practice various forms of self-mutilation (see, for example, 1 Kings 18:26-29) the Hebrews were never allowed to forget that only vicarious sacrifice had any power to cleanse and purify. Coupled with burning, the sprinkling or splashing of the blood became the symbol of the justification and sanctification of the individual, possible only through the sacrifice of another.

> The relation which the sprinkling of the blood and the burning of the flesh of the sacrifice upon the altar bore to one another was that of justification and sanctification, those two indispensable conditions, without which sinful man could not attain to reconciliation with God and life in God. But as the sinner could neither justify himself before God nor sanctify himself by his own power, the sprinkling of blood and the burning of the portions of the sacrifice upon

the altar were to be effected, not by the offerer himself, but only by the priest, as the mediator whom God had chosen and sanctified, not only that the soul which had been covered by the sacrificial blood might thereby be brought to God and received into His favour, but also that the bodily members, of which the flesh of the sacrifice was a symbol, might be given up to the fire of the Holy Spirit, to be purified and sanctified from the dross of sin, and raised in a glorified state to God; just as the sacrificial gift was consumed in the altar fire, so that, whilst its earthly perishable elements were turned into ashes and left behind, its true essence ascended towards heaven, where God is enthroned, in the most ethereal and glorified of material forms, as a sweet-smelling savour, *i.e.* as an acceptable offering. (Keil and Delitzsch, 1:280-81.)

Sin Offering   Leviticus 4:4-5, 13; 16:24-30

Two offerings fit into the category of sin offerings, and both were demanded by the law for forgiveness of sins. Because they were to precede the other kind of offerings (i.e., "sweet savor") they also were referred to as preparatory. It is important not to confuse the sin offering proper with the general category called sin offerings. It is the sin offering proper to which we now turn our attention. This offering was suited to the station and circumstance of the person offering it: the high priest and the congregation of Israel were required to offer a young bull — a prince brought a he-goat, while a commoner could bring a she-goat or lamb. If he was destitute, he could bring two pigeons or turtledoves. One of these, however, served as a burnt offering. In extreme cases a tenth of an *ephah* of flour was permitted.

The offerer brought the animal to the temple, placed his hands on its head, thus identifying himself with the animal and symbolically transferring his own sins to it. It was then sacrificed on the north side of the altar. The high priest collected the blood, placed some of it on the horns of the altar, and poured the rest out at its base. The blood of birds was splashed on the sides of the altar. On the Day of Atonement the blood was manipulated differently. (Since this was a special case, it will be treated later under the section on festivals.) The portion of the entrails viewed as delicacies (the two kidneys with their fat and the appendage to the liver) were consumed upon the altar. This was also true of any flour offering as well as one of the two birds offered by the poor. The carcass of the bull (everything but those delicacies already burned at the altar), which was sacrificed for the high priest, his family, and the house of Israel, was carried outside the camp to a designated spot and burned. With the exception of this bull and the one dove of the poor, the edible portion of the sacrificial animals became the property of the officiating priest for food.

The objective of the sin offering was forgiveness. This was not for any particular sin, but rather for those which spring from the weaknesses of the flesh and those which were committed unknowingly or unintentionally. Thus, the sprinkling of the blood takes on great importance. The lesson is clear. It is only through the blood shed by the Christ that man's fallen nature can be changed and overcome so that he can become a son of God and thereby obtain perfection. (Compare Mosiah 5:2-7; Romans 6:1-7; Mosiah 3:19; 1 John 2:1-3; 3:1-2, 9; 5:8.)

That God would allow grains to be used as an acceptable offering teaches two important principles. First, since the offering was obligatory, Jehovah's mercy allowed all, no matter what their station, abilities, or talents, to make an acceptable sacrifice. Indeed, because of the Atonement, the mercy of the Savior extends to each individual so that he is judged only against himself. Thus, the door of salvation is closed against no one. Second, it stresses the idea that all sacrifices are vicarious in nature, the grain actually serving as a vicarious offering for the blood. Again, this points to the indispensible vicarious atonement of the Lord.

The north side of the altar, where all animals except those used for the peace offering were sacrificed, was nearest to the door of the tabernacle or temple (the dwelling place of God), thus suggesting that no one can approach deity without first sacrificing all worldliness. The major lesson one learns from this sacrifice however is that every transgression of God's laws, whether committed in ignorance or not, must be atoned for. The life of the offering was given to pay for sin—even ignorant sin. The carcass of the ox (minus those "delicacies" already burnt on the altar) was not burnt upon the altar. It was given up to destruction by fire outside of the camp. This may have been partly because it was sacrificed in behalf of not only the whole congregation but also of the chief priests and their families who were, themselves, a class of vicarious servants who ceremoniously accepted responsibility for the sins of the people. We note that Jesus was crucified outside the city wall. So there are some great analogies to be drawn between the sacrifice of the Savior and the fate of the ox who symbolized Jesus and who was burned outside the camp.

Trespass Offering   Leviticus 5:14-16; 7:1-10

As noted above, the trespass offering was in the general class of sin offerings. The ritual of this sacrifice followed closely that of the sin offering outlined above, though in this case the law did not allow for substitute offerings.

Almost universally a ram was required. Further, the priest placed none of the blood on the horns of the altar but sprinkled it only about the base of the altar. The outstanding feature of this sacrifice was the placing of a monetary value upon the ram by the officiating priest. The value was set in accordance with the degree of the trespass committed by the individual. The animal was then sacrificed, the prescribed portions being burnt upon the altar and the rest going to the priest. The individual making the offering was then required to give to the individual he had offended the prescribed price and an additional 20 percent.

The objective of the trespass offering was to gain forgiveness of sins knowingly committed. Confession, restoration, and/or satisfaction of the rights or goods which had been violated or disturbed were required before the blood could cleanse one from sin. The law named specific sins which demanded expiation in this manner: (1) being unfaithful in the payment of tithes and offerings; (2) violating oaths or becoming ceremonially unclean during the time of oaths, thus depriving God of service or time which was promised him (for this offense the ram without an additional value added was deemed satisfactory); and, (3) crimes against one's neighbors arising out of avarice, selfishness and false swearing.

The lesson appears to be that the blood of Christ, though freely given for sins committed in ignorance, will not cover those committed knowingly unless the individual willingly and contritely confesses, makes restitution where possible, and forsakes his sins.

Burnt Offering   Leviticus 1:3-17; 6:8-13

The burnt offering was by far the most frequent sacrifice at the Hebrew sanctuaries. The law allowed a bull, goat, sheep, or bird to be acceptable, again according to the financial circumstance of the individual. As with all blood sacrifices, the offerer placed his hands upon the animal's head and then slaughtered it. The priest collected the blood and sprinkled it around the altar. In the case of birds, he pinched the neck and drained the blood on the side of the altar. The offerer, in the meantime, skinned the animal and dissected it as prescribed, and washed the unclean portions. These were then taken by the priest and carefully arranged upon the altar and burned. The ascending smoke was intended to be a pleasing odor (translated ''sweet savor'' in the King James Bible) unto the Lord.

As with the sin offerings, the purpose of the burnt offering was expiation. The idea behind the burnt offering, however, was self-surrender to God for the purpose of securing divine acceptance and favor. Therefore, it would appear that the ritual of laying the hand on the animal's head was for a different purpose than that of the sin offerings. This time the rite was attended to with a prayer of dedication by which the individual symbolically imputed to the animal his noble desires, intents and feelings. By this means, it was made pleasing or satisfying to Jehovah. The animal, being the product of the man's efforts, made a good symbol of his time, or life, and substance. In this way he was presenting his whole life before the Lord that it might be sanctified by Him. This is expressed particularly in the dividing of the animal into head, legs, fat and inwards: The head was a symbol of the mind and intellect, the legs of freewill and power, the inwards of the emotions, and the fat of health and well being. The whole, therefore, symbolized consecration necessary to achieve power unto eternal life.

The priest acted, as always, as the mediator between the yet sinful man and God. Only the priest could offer the vicarious blood through which the offerer was not only forgiven but reconciled. The fire in the altar represented the Holy Spirit's power to purge, cleanse, and purify the sincere individual. But the cleansing was possible only after the blood was shed. Thus, this ordinance reveals the role of Christ as mediator and reconciler preparing the way for the sanctifying actions of the Holy Spirit.

Peace Offering   Leviticus 3:1-17; 7:11-34

In Hebrew the name of the peace offering takes the plural form. This is fitting since there were a number of sacrifices — thanks, praise, vow, and freewill offerings — which followed essentially the same form but were offered for different, though related, purposes.

The presentation of the animal as well as the laying on of hands was the same as in the sin offering. As noted earlier, however, the animal was not slaughtered on the north side of the altar but, rather, at the door between the inner and outer court. The law allowed any domestic animal from the herd or flock, regardless of gender, to be used, provided it met the physical criteria. Birds were not allowed, however. The priest both sprinkled and splashed the blood on all sides of the altar. Those entrails considered as delicacies, along with the fat tail of the sheep, were burnt on the altar. The law dictated that this be done only after the burnt offering had been made.

For his part, the priest received the brisket, referred to as the "wave offering," and the right leg, called the "heave offering." The former was received through the ritual of waving, wherein the breast piece was placed in the hands of the offerer with the priest's hands under his. The offering was then moved in a horizontal motion toward the altar then back again. This act signified offering the piece to Jehovah, his acceptance, and its transference to his priest.

The rest of the flesh was taken by the offerer to his home where he prepared a feast with it for his family and friends, sharing a portion with the poor. None of the meat was to be allowed to spoil, the law requiring any remaining portions to be burned by the second day.

As the name suggests, the purpose of the peace offering was to establish or give thanks for peace and salvation. In making the sacrifice, the offerer signified that he gave up earthly things in order to partake of heavenly things. This would serve to strengthen and nourish his body and soul as he walked in holy ways. That portion of the animal received back by the offerer became a symbol of this spiritual nourishment which was made possible only through the great and last sacrifice of the Lord. The meal then became a celebration of the successful sacrifice of Christ through which one received the eternal blessings of life and joy. In this way, it was a covenant meal representing domestic fellowship with the Lord, the earthly food symbolizing the spiritual power through which the Lord satisfies and refreshes his Saints.

Meat Offering   Leviticus 2:1-16; 6:14-18

The name of the meat offering might make better sense if it were translated "cereal" or "grain" offering. *Meat* in King James language means *food*. The Hebrew name for this offering could be translated "fruit of the ground." The law stated that three types of "meat" or food were acceptable: (1) fine flour, oil, salt, and incense; (2) pastries made of fine flour, oil, and salt and excluding honey and leaven — these could be baked, boiled, or pan-fried in oil; and, (3) as a "first fruits" offering, parched or roasted kernels with salt, oil, and incense. This latter category could also include bread made with leaven and honey. This, however, could not be offered upon the altar.

The offerer brought the offering to the priest and poured oil over a portion of it. The priest then took a handful of the flour, unleavened bread, or grains, over which the oil had been poured, along with salt and all of the incense, and offered them upon the altar. The remaining portion along with all the leavened bread became the property of the priest.

In the meat offering the Israelite was truly offering his daily bread. In doing so, he expressed a desire that by giving up the temporal, he might be filled with the spiritual. Indeed, the Lord is the bread of life who will cause all men who partake thereof to never hunger. (See John 6:35.) In symbolic representation of that life, all grains had to be prepared some way. The highest offering was of finely ground flour. It is interesting that the threshing sledge and mill wheel are called the *tribulum,* from which comes the word *tribulation.* It was because of the tribulation which the Lord endured that he was an acceptable sacrifice.

In addition to the prepared grains, three other ingredients need to be noted: the salt, oil, and incense. The incense was symbolic of prayer through which one's life was dedicated to God and thus became well pleasing. Salt was used anciently as a preservative as well as a savor (flavor enhancer). When used with a sacrifice it was called the "salt of the covenant," suggesting that it is through making and keeping covenants that spiritual life is sustained. The oil represented the Holy Ghost, which is given to all those who make and keep covenants. This was poured over or kneaded into the wheat. The scriptures use wheat as the symbol for the word of God. This ordinance clearly revealed that as wheat and oil nourish and strengthen the physical man, so the word and spirit serve to strengthen the inner man.

BIBLICAL FESTIVALS

The Mosaic sacrifices repeatedly called attention to Christ and the importance of his atonement. The message was difficult to miss: Only through the blood of the Lamb can one become clean, acceptable to God, receive the spirit, and partake of eternal life. The sacrifices just described were associated directly with certain festivals or holy days. They, too, afforded an opportunity to gain insight into the life and mission of the Lord.

The main and regular biblical festivals that were commanded by God were the following: Sabbath, New Moon, Passover, Feast of Tabernacles, Pentecost, and the Day of Atonement. These festivals were to be characterized by (1) special sacrificial services, (2) special ceremonies such as the ritual meal at Passover, and (3) rejoicing before the Lord. It was intended that on these days man would cease from his labors and celebrate a communion with Jehovah, partaking of the abundance of the field or flock which he had so graciously provided. The effects of the Fall, by which man was to eat bread by the sweat of his brow, were, so to speak, temporarily suspended, God supplying the meals out of his share. This allowed his children to devote themselves totally to the enjoyment of the association of his Spirit.

Passover   Exodus 12:1-28

The Passover was essentially a festival of remembrance. It looked back to the days of Egyptian bondage and the power of God which freed Israel from servitude. It is interesting that this feast was first celebrated by direction of Jehovah, before the children of Israel were delivered from bondage. The reason for this is apparently twofold: first, to assure that Israel never forgot what God had done in allowing the angel of death to pass over the house of Israel; second, to prepare them for their adoption as the nation of Jehovah. As they were about to be severed from physical bondage, they were also to sever themselves from heathen idolatry and consecrate themselves to the Lord. This consecration was to be made through the celebration of the Passover—a festival which marked the birth of the nation of Israel. Therefore, it was from its celebration that the Hebrews marked their new year.

The Passover centered in the sacrifice of the Paschal Lamb. Chosen three days before, the lamb of each family or group was brought to the temple and sacrificed about sunset. The priest sprinkled some of the blood upon the altar, after which the family prepared the lamb and the accompanying meal. The lamb was to be roasted in such a way that no bones were broken. Unleavened bread and bitter herbs also were eaten. At least a portion of the meal was eaten while standing and wearing sandals.

Each part of the meal had meaning: The standing position, the wearing of sandals, and the unleavened bread suggested haste; the bitter herbs symbolized bondage; and the lamb personified the grace of God by which Israel was saved. Egypt was often used in the scriptures as a symbol of the world of sin. As Israel was only released from servitude therein through the death of the Egyptian firstborn, so could she free herself from the wages of sin only through the death of the firstborn of God and by partaking of his Spirit. The lamb, being separated from the flock for three days and then providing the ransoming blood, symbolized the Lord who was separated from life for three days before breaking the bands of death and providing the way for all to escape. As the lamb provided the physical energy which Israel found necessary to escape the physical bondage of Egypt, so, too, the Spirit of Christ provided the strength necessary to flee the spiritual bondage they were in. And this symbolism still carries a message today for those who seek to escape the bondage of Babylon and find the freedom of Zion.

Feast of Tabernacles   Exodus 23:16; 34:22

The Feast of Tabernacles was celebrated at the ingathering of wheat and grapes. It was one of the most important celebrations of the Hebrews and was called "the feast of the Lord" (see Leviticus 23:39), and it was marked by the construction of booths in which the Israelites dwelt during the week-long celebration. The prominent object of the feast was the festival of joy, which celebrated the harvest and Israel's release from Egyptian bondage. The booths or "tabernacles" were a symbol of the tents in which the tribes of Israel dwelt during their wanderings in the wilderness. The sacrifices prescribed by the law for this feast were more numerous than for any other. A distin-

guishing feature was the recitation of the ''Psalm of En-
thronement.'' (Psalm 47:93, 96-99.)

The elaborate sacrifices offered in connection with the
celebration of the harvest stress that all good things come
from God and are made possible because of the atonement
of the Lord. It is through him that men are made free,
escaping the world of sin and being allowed to dwell, so to
speak, in the tabernacle of God. But there was something
more to this feast: The recitation of the Psalms and the
rituals associated therewith were symbolic of the crowning
of Jehovah as King. The festival of joy, then, was the celebration of the beginning of the kingdom of God. As the
Passover looked back, the Feast of Tabernacles looked forward. It was a royal Zion feast in anticipation of the day
when Christ would be crowned and reign as Lord of lords
and King of kings.

Pentecost   Exodus 34:22; Deuteronomy 16:10

Pentecost might be said to be an additional one-day
feast of Passover since its celebration was marked fifty days
after the Sabbath of the Passover week. (Leviticus 23:15-
16.) This usually came at the end of the barley harvest and
the beginning of the wheat harvest. Therefore, it was considered a celebration of first fruits. Though the length of the
celebration was later expanded, initially it was a one-day
feast of thanksgiving. On this day, in addition to sacrificial
rites, the new meal offering was waved before the altar of the
Lord. This consisted of two loaves of bread made of the
finest wheat grown that year. In addition, the law encouraged offerings of ''sweet savor'' or free-will offerings.

Like the Feast of Tabernacles, this celebration was a
reminder that all good things come from God through

Christ. Therefore, as God sustained man, so man was to dedicate himself to God.

Day of Atonement Leviticus 16:1-34

The most important day of the liturgical year was the Day of Atonement. It was on this day that all the sins of the whole house of Israel were purged. It was called a Sabbath of solemn rest, and in it every soul was to humble himself before the Lord through fasting and prayer. Thus, it stands in marked contrast to all the other feasts which were times of rejoicing. On this day solemnity was to rule that Israel might continually keep in mind the seriousness of the purgation taking place in its behalf.

The sacrificial order of the day was precisely spelled out. The high priest was to offer a bull for a sin offering and a ram for a burnt offering for himself and his household. Then he was to offer two male goats for a sin offering and a ram for a burnt offering for all of Israel. One of the goats, chosen by lot, was not slaughtered but retained for a special purpose which will be explained below.

The first task of the high priest, after making the sacrifices, was the cleansing of the tabernacle or temple, believed necessary because not all who came there to worship did so for the right reason. Any wantonness, rebellion, or hypocrisy defiled the temple and its court. To cleanse the house of the Lord, the high priest bathed, put on special white linen garments, and made the sacrifice for himself. He then took incense, a censer of living coals from the altar, and a bowl of the sacrificial blood into the Holy of Holies. After burning incense in the censer, he sprinkled some of the blood seven times upon the front of the mercy seat. After this, he returned to the altar, sacrificed the sin offering

for the house of Israel, and brought that blood into the
Holy of Holies, where it too was sprinkled seven times upon
the mercy seat. Next he went into the holy place where he
sprinkled the blood from both offerings upon the veil. After
this he returned to the altar, combined the blood of the sacrifices, placed some on the altar's horns and seven times
sprinkled some blood upon it. The number seven sym-
bolizes the covenant relationship between God and Israel.
The sprinkling of the blood suggested that only as Israel
kept the covenants could God dwell in her midst. If the
covenant was broken, only repentance and atonement could
bring the Spirit back.

Once the Lord's house was cleansed, the high priest
turned his attention to the house of Israel. He called for the
goat which, at the time the lots were cast, had had placed
around its neck a scarlet ribbon designating it as the "scapegoat." Placing his hands upon its head, the high priest
confessed all the sins of Israel. This was a ritual confession
and not an attempt to enumerate each and every sin. The
goat was then taken by a strong man and led out into the
Judean wilderness to perish. After this, the high priest
washed and changed into his high priestly apparel and
offered the burnt offerings upon the altar.

In the activities of this day, one is again struck by the
powerful symbols used to convey the message. All sin must
be atoned for, some by blood, some by a recompense, and
some by ostricism or banishment. Those sins heaped upon
the scapegoat centered in rebellion. The consequence of
such, if not repented of, would be eternal banishment from
the kingdom of God. (Some have seen the "scapegoat" as a
type of Satan and his banishment to perdition.) But once
Israel was clean, she could then make that sacrifice which
made her acceptable to the Lord.

LESSONS TO BE DRAWN

Continually the Lord sought to bring Israel to him through the law of performances and ordinances. Those with eyes enlightened by the spirit of prophecy were taught through these activities the importance of the mission of Christ, how and why they could have their sins remitted, and how they could make their lives acceptable to the Lord. The great festivals were reminders that faith and trust in God brought great blessings, including the abundance of the earth. Indeed, for those who would keep the covenant there would be joy in this world and eternal life in the world to come.

> But behold, the Jews were a stiffnecked people; and they despised the words of plainness, and killed the prophets, and sought for things that they could not understand. Wherefore, because of their blindness, which blindness came by looking beyond the mark, they must needs fall; for God hath taken away his plainness from them, and delivered unto them many things which they cannot understand, because they desired it. And because they desired it God hath done it, that they may stumble.
>
> And now I, Jacob, am led on by the Spirit unto prophesying; for I perceive by the workings of the Spirit which is in me, that by the stumbling of the Jews they will reject the stone upon which they might build and have safe foundation.
>
> But behold, according to the scriptures, this stone shall become the great, and the last, and the only sure foundation, upon which the Jews can build. (Jacob 4:14-16.)

One last lesson may be drawn from a study of the sacrifices and celebrations of the law of Moses. A loss of time and materials — wealth — went into them. From a strictly rational point of view, the Israelites would have been wealthier without this great waste of time and food. But that is not the case. When the spiritual and emotional life is properly nourished and tended, the physical life prospers too. We all need to learn that we needn't spend all our time in work, in the pursuit of wealth or material happiness and security. Security is in the goodness and largesse of God. Happiness is in righteousness. Most of the Israelites did not learn that. But their lives and their laws were not for them alone. We can learn from a study of their lives and of their mistakes. We can put our lives in order so that there is a balance there. Above all, we can learn that Christ is the foundation stone on which we build and from which all else that is good grows.

6

Understanding the Old Testament

Probably the greatest enemy to understanding the Old Testament is the inertia that most people experience when facing any worthwhile but difficult task. In other words, just getting on with it may be the most important step towards understanding it. A great stake president, whose stake led the Church in many statistics, had a wise answer to those critics who said that quality home teaching was more important than having a record of 100 percent home teaching. He said: "That is very true. However, I don't see how you can have quality home teaching if you don't go at all. Any home that is missed won't have any kind of home teaching whatever. It all begins with getting to every home, and getting there does not constitute poor home teaching. It is the beginning of good home teaching."

To paraphrase him a little: "You certainly cannot begin to understand the Old Testament until you begin to read it. No amount of looking at it on the shelf or of reading about what others have said about it will be of much value until you have read it yourself at least one time. Those who really understand it have read the Book of Mormon many times and the Old Testament at least a few times. Then they have consulted the experts.''

At about fourteen years of age President Spencer W. Kimball read the Bible as a result of a challenge by Suza Young Gates. At a stake conference near his home in Thatcher, Arizona, Sister Gates asked the congregation how many had read the Bible. Only five or six hands went up in a congregation of about a thousand. He walked home and commenced the project that she challenged them all to do. A year later he finished. He did not understand all of the Bible, but he plowed through and finished—a great accomplishment for a teenager. And he *began* to understand. He must have read much of it many times after that, for his conference addresses are liberally sprinkled with Old Testament quotations all through the years. And his use of these quotations shows great understanding.

There are very few adults in the Church who could give a good reason for not having read the Old Testament. By reading a few pages a day, each of the standard works can be read in a year. One stake president read the standard works once a year during the last twenty-five years of his life. In addition to being a stake president, he was principal of a high school during much of this time. So he was a very busy man. This program had a profound effect on his life and, no doubt, on the lives of many others. There are very few things a Latter-day Saint can do that can have a greater influence for good on him or her and for correct thinking than reading the scriptures constantly.

READING FOR COMPREHENSION

The King James Bible is a reasonably literal translation — even to the point of being clumsy in English in some places in order to maintain that literalness rather than resorting to paraphrasing and interpreting. There are some newer translations which have attempted to make reading the Bible easier. They are not as true to the texts, however. For practical reasons that involve missionary work and standardization the Latter-day Saint will want to conquer the King James Version. The solution is to read until the language becomes familiar. Following are some illustrations that show the difference in the meaning as opposed to the literal wording of the King James translation:

1. King James: ". . . Yea, hath God said, Ye shall not eat of every tree of the garden?" (Genesis 3:1.)

Clarification: Is it true that God has forbidden you to eat from any tree of the garden whatsoever? (Or, possibly, Is it true God has said you must not eat of some of the trees of the garden.)

2. ". . . Am I my brother's keeper?" (Genesis 4:9.)

Clarification: Am I my brother's jailer? (That is, "Should I be responsible for everything my brother does?" This seems to have been a pot-shot at the doctrine of free agency, which Cain had repudiated.)

3. "The heart of her husband doth safely trust in her, so that he will have no need for spoil." (Proverbs 31:11.)

Clarification: Her husband knows that she will never create a situation that will make it necessary for him to brawl over her or to go to court to seek restitution.

4. "Is there anything whereof it may be said, See, this is new? it hath been already of old time, which was before us." (Ecclesiastes 1:10.)

Clarification: Is there anything whereof it may be said, "See, this is new?" No. Whatever it is, the same thing has happened long before our times.

5. "Also take no heed unto all words that are spoken; lest thou hear thy servant curse thee: For oftentimes also thine own heart knoweth that thou thyself likewise hast cursed others." (Ecclesiastes 7: 21, 22.)

Clarification: Don't try to find out if your employees are saying evil about you. You may hear one of them curse you. And you really know that this is meaningless, because you have often done the same thing yourself when you really didn't mean it.

6. ". . . Who shall declare his generation? for he was cut off out of the land of the living. . . ." (Isaiah 53:8.)

Clarification: Who shall give the names of the descendants he could have generated if he had not died so young?

The above clarified readings are, of course, personal interpretations to some extent. It is hoped that they are not private (2 Peter 1:20), but of the Spirit. But all reading involves interpretation or understanding. It is just that some readings are so simple and clear that almost any number of reasonable and knowing people would agree on the meaning. But others are more difficult. Probably no two Old Testament scholars would agree on the meaning of every verse. But the Saints can agree with each other on most of the Old Testament if they all work hard enough. The point is that they must work at it. After a period of consistent study, a person can come to *know* that he knows. It is similar to geometry. One knows for sure that he is right when he is right. He has applied the correct theorem, which solved the problem, and he knew his answer was correct without checking with anyone else. He positively knew it and knew that he knew it. With this knowledge there is a feeling in the heart and mind that is very much like, if not identical to, the feeling one has when he knows that he has understood a difficult passage of scripture. What is more, he does not forget it. He knows it the next time he comes to it. And it expands his mind and expands the quantity and improves the quality of the rest of his scriptural and theological understanding. (See D&C 50:17-24.)

A good share of the intellectual work involved in understanding the Bible is the same as would be involved in understanding anything else. So a knowledge of grammar and a good vocabulary are useful. A Bible dictionary is useful to solve vocabulary problems; but there is no easy way to master grammar if it was not done while attending school. Copious reading is probably the best teacher, if the reading is of a good quality and requires thought. Also, those who write frequently—such as in a journal and letters to friends—improve their knowledge of grammar, if they conscientiously try to write correctly and refer to grammar texts for help.

PICKING UP TIME CUES

The Old Testament prophets are the hardest of all the books of the Bible to understand, primarily because of the prophecies in their writings. One reason the prophecies are hard to understand is that the time when the prophecy is to be fulfilled usually has to be deduced. Rarely is a date given. Jeremiah once foretold that the duration of the Babylonian captivity would be seventy years. (Jeremiah 25:11.) Even then, he did not fix the beginning and ending date. Consequently there has been much speculation in the commentaries as to just when the seventy years began and ended. But in this case, the date isn't crucial—just about any reasonable calculation will show that he was right. Time is very important in many other prophecies, however. Following are some illustrations of kinds of time cues and how they appear:

1. Jeremiah 3:18: "In those days the house of Judah shall walk with the house of Israel, and they shall come together out of the land of the north to the land that I have given for an inheritance unto your fathers."

In this passage there are some very typical prophetic time cues. First, the reader must remember that the ten tribes (here called Israel) had been lost in "the north countries" for over one hundred years. And it had been prophesied that they would remain lost until the great restoration of Israel and Judah in the last days. Hence, we know immediately that this prophecy refers to the time shortly before the Millennium—our time and later. And, since it has not all been fulfilled—even though Latter-day Saints know that its fulfillment has commenced—we can deduce that it is to be finished in the not-too-distant future. Another cue is the expression "in those days." More often than not this expression refers to the last days—our day.

In this case, the context clearly establishes that it has reference to our day. Adam Clarke (4:262) is somewhat confused. He would like to give it a dual or triple meaning. Erroneously he ties it to the return from Babylon. But this was from the east, not from the north. And Israel was not there, nor did she return from there. Only Judah was in Babylon, and not even all of Judah returned. His next suggestion—that it may refer to Jesus' day—was equally incorrect, because no such return of Israel occurred. In addition, the Jews had not yet been scattered into the north countries in Jesus' day. Later they were. Millions are still in Russia, America, all the rest of the north countries, and in "all the coasts of the earth" (see, for example, Jeremiah 31:8) in the same places we are finding the rest of Israel. Clarke's third choice is very close in that he ties it, finally, to a date future to his time (the 1820s), except that he does not understand who Israel is. His interpretation is that Israel is a metaphor for the Christians of a particular Protestant persuasion.

2. Isaiah 28: Since Israel had not yet gone into captivity (Isaiah 28 is dated at 725 B.C. by Usher's calculations as cited in Clarke, 4:122), this prophecy might refer to ancient Israel. It does not, however—though it has some dual characteristics. The time cues clearly show that the prophet was warning modern Israel. These cues are: First, "the Lord hath a mighty and strong one. . . ." This is an event associated with the establishment of the latter-day Zion. (See also D&C 85:7.) Second, verse five speaks of a residue that will be preserved from among the "drunkards of Ephraim" (verse 3). No such residue was preserved in antiquity. The Savior did not become "a crown of glory" or "a diadem of beauty" to any part of Ephraim in Isaiah's day or from then to now. This latter-day cleansing of Ephraim is yet to come. (See D&C 112:24-26.) Third, verse five also uses "in that day" in a manner that ties the time to the other latter-day events described. And there are other time cues in Isaiah 28 for the careful reader.

3. Isaiah 29: This chapter covers a long sweep of

history. We would not be able to put it all together if it weren't for the following facts: We know about some of the events that already have occurred; 2 Nephi 26 and 27 are, to a great extent, an inspired commentary on Isaiah 29; and we have scores of pages of commentary from modern prophets. The chapter itself contains some interesting clues, however. For instance, verse 17 is a dead giveaway. This statement can refer only to an event that is to shortly precede or go into the Millennium. So, the day of the book and those related events is to be at a time that is "yet a very little while" before the Millennium. Also, verse 18 has one of those "in that day" cues accompanied by a list of events (verses 18 to 24) that are occurring now or will occur shortly. Finally, verses 22 and 23 tell us that the time under discussion is to end with Jacob's final great triumph when his posterity are to be restored to a worship of Christ, who is here called the "God of Israel" and "the Holy One of Jacob." This is in the process of fulfillment and will culminate in those events that follow Jesus' appearance on the Mount of Olives when it splits in two under his feet and brings forth from the temple area the great stream of water that will flow through and sweeten the Dead Sea. Then "Jacob shall not now be ashamed, neither shall his face now wax pale" (verse 22). The reason is that only then will a whole nation of Jews be converted. (See D&C 45:50-59. Compare verse 50 to Isaiah 29:20.)

INTERPRETING THE FIGURATIVE

The first lesson in interpreting figurative passages is that figurative passages are meant to be taken just as literally as literal passages. That is to say, the writer means them just as much. They are just as important, maybe more so. And, when they are understood, they are just as literal as any other passage. It is that literal meaning behind the figurative meaning that the reader should seek.

Consider for example the brazen serpent that Moses was told to put on a staff in the wilderness when the Israelites had been bitten by fiery, flying serpents. (Numbers 21:5-9.) This serpent of brass on the staff represented Jesus upon the cross; the flying serpents represented sin; looking upon the brass serpent represented faith in Christ; being healed represented salvation. The event was real: The people were bitten; they died; some were healed and some were not. An actual brass serpent was raised up on a staff, and so on. The Lord used this whole event to teach a lesson about the Savior, however. This lesson about the Savior and his healing power was just as real as the experience of being bitten and healed there in the wilderness. (See also the Book of Mormon explanations of this event in 1 Nephi 17:41; 2 Nephi 25:20; and Helaman 8:14-15.)

One reason why the figurative language of the Old Testament is at first a little hard to understand is that it comes out of another time from a culture that is different in some ways—especially those involving language. But one only needs to become familiar with the common figures of speech used repeatedly by the Jews to begin to understand much of this manner of writing. And even where the figurative language may not be understood, one still can tell that it is figurative. And, knowing that, he knows what he must try to do to understand the passage.

When Adam Clarke wrote his introduction to the book of Isaiah, he quoted copiously from a tract called *A Summary*

View and Explanation of the Writings of the Prophets, written
in 1804 by Dr. John Smith of Cambleton. It is so amazingly
correct that one cannot help but admire the devotion to
Jehovah which he and other scholars of England and Scot-
land in that day must have had. It helps explain why so
many British people embraced the gospel as soon as it
was restored. These scholars followed the same general
spiritual maturity and fidelity of the King James translators.
Dr. Smith's remarks are so helpful that much of what he
said is reproduced below, as quoted by Adam Clarke, with
some comments of the present author interspersed.

>   "The writings of the prophets, the most sublime and
> beautiful in the world, lose much of that usefulness and
> effect which they are so well calculated to produce on the
> souls of men, from their not being more generally under-
> stood. Many prophecies are somewhat dark, till events
> explain them. They are, besides, delivered in such lofty
> and figurative terms, and with such frequent allusions to the
> customs and manners of times and places the most remote,
> that ordinary readers cannot, without some help, be sup-
> posed capable of understanding them. It must therefore
> be of use to make the language of prophecy as intelligible
> as may be, by explaining those images and figures of speech
> in which it most frequently abounds; and this may be done
> generally, even when the prophecies themselves are obscure.
>   "Some prophecies seem as if it were not intended that
> they should be clearly understood before they are fulfilled.
> As they relate to different periods, they may have been
> intended for exciting the attention of mankind from time
> to time both to providence and to Scripture and to furnish
> every age with new evidence of Divine revelation; by which
> means they serve the same purpose to the last ages of the
> world that miracles did to the first. Whereas, if they had
> been in every respect clear and obvious from the beginning,
> this wise purpose had been in a great measure defeated.

Curiosity, industry, and attention would at once be at an end, or, by being too easily gratified, would be little exercised.

"Besides, a great degree of obscurity is necessary to some prophecies before they can be fulfilled; and if not fulfilled, the consequence would not be so beneficial to mankind. Thus many of the ancient prophecies concerning the destruction of Jerusalem had a manifest relation to the remoter destruction by the Romans, as well as to the nearer one by the Chaldeans. Had the Jews perceived this, which was not indeed clear enough till the event explained it, they would probably have wished to have remained for ever in their captivity at Babylon, rather than expose themselves or their offspring a second time to a destruction so dreadful as that which they had already experienced.

An example that illustrates the assertion in the last paragraph above can be found in Leviticus 26 and Deuteronomy 28. There are many events foretold there by Moses that were fulfilled more than once, sometimes more than twice. For example, he foretold that if the Israelites were untrue to the covenant they would be reduced to cannibalism. (Leviticus 26:29; Deuteronomy 28:53-57.) This was fulfilled in the Babylonian siege of Jerusalem in the days of Zedekiah and during the Roman siege of Jerusalem. And it was fulfilled in the years that followed the downfall of the Nephite civilization, as recorded, for example, in Moroni 9:8.

"With respect to our times, by far the greatest number of prophecies relate to events which are now past; and therefore a sufficient acquaintance with history, and with the language and style of prophecy, is all that is requisite to understand them. Some prophecies, however, relate to events still future; and these too may be understood in general, although some particular circumstances connected with them may remain obscure till they are fulfilled. If prophecies were not capable of being understood in general, we should not find the Jews so often blamed in this respect for their ignorance and want of discernment. That they did actually understand many of them when they chose to search the Scriptures we know. Daniel understood, from the prophecies of Jeremiah, the time at which the captivity in Babylon was to be at an end; and the scribes knew from Micah, and told Herod, where the Messiah was to be born. A very little attention might have enabled them in the same manner to understand others, as they probably did; such as the seventy weeks of Daniel; the destruction of the Babylonian empire, and of the other three that were to succeed; and also of the ruin of the people and places around them, Moab, Ammon, Tyre, Sidon, Philistia, Egypt, and Idumea. Perhaps, indeed, a few enigmatical circumstances might have been annexed, which could not be understood till they were accomplished; but the general tenor of the prophecies they could be at no loss to understand. With regard to prophecies still future, we are in a similar situation. It is understood in general, that the Jews will be gathered from their dispersions, restored to their own land, and converted to Christianity; that the fulness of the Gentiles will likewise come in; that Antichrist, Gog and Magog, and all the enemies of the Church will be destroyed; after which the Gospel will remarkably flourish, and be more than ever glorified. But several circumstances connected with those general events must probably remain in the dark till their accomplishment shall clearly explain them.

A year after Dr. Smith made this prediction Joseph Smith was born, and these events began to unfold so that the gospel could "remarkably flourish."

"But this degree of obscurity which sometimes attends prophecy does not always proceed from the circumstances or subject; it frequently proceeds from the highly poetical and figurative style, in which prophecy is for the most part conveyed, and of which it will be proper to give some account. To speak of all the rhetorical figures with which the prophets adorn their style would lead us into a field too wide, and would be more the province of the rhetorician than of the commentator. It will be sufficient for our purpose at present to attend to the most common of them, consisting of *allegory, parable,* and *metaphor,* and then to consider the *sources* from which the prophets most frequently borrow their images in those figures, and the sense which they wish to convey by them.

"By *allegory,* the first of the figures mentioned, is meant that mode of speech in which the writer or speaker means to convey a different idea from what the words in their obvious and primary signification bear. Thus, 'Break up your fallow ground, and sow not among thorns,' (Jer. iv. 3,) is to be understood, not of *tillage,* but of *repentance.* And these words, 'Thy rowers have brought thee into great waters, the east wind hath broken thee in the midst of the seas,' Ezek. xxvii. 26, allude not to the fate of a *ship,* but of a *city.*

"To this figure the *parable,* in which the prophets frequently speak, is nearly allied. It consists in the application of some feigned narrative to some real truth, which might have been less striking or more disagreeable if expressed in plain terms. Such is the following one of Isaiah, v. 1, 2: 'My well-beloved hath a vineyard in a very fruitful hill. And he fenced it, and gathered out the stones thereof, and planted it with the choicest vine, and built a tower in the midst of it, and also made a wine-press therein; and he looked that it should bring forth grapes, and it brought forth wild grapes.' The seventh verse tells us that this *vineyard* was the *house of Israel,* which had so ill requited the favour which God had shown it.

"There is, besides, another kind of allegory not uncommon with the prophets, called *mystical allegory* or *double prophecy.* Thus it is said of Eliakim, Isa. xxii. 22: 'And the key of the house of David will I lay upon his shoulder; and he shall open, and none shall shut; and he shall shut, and none shall open.' In the first and obvious sense, the words

relate to Eliakim; but in the secondary or mystical sense,
to the Messiah. Instances of the same kind are frequent in
those prophecies that relate to David, Zerubbabel, Cyrus,
and other types of Christ. In the first sense the words relate
to the type; in the second, to the antitype. The use of this
allegory, however, is not so frequent as that of the former.
It is generally confined to things most nearly connected with
the Jewish religion; with Israel, Sion, Jerusalem, and its
kings and rulers; or such as were most opposite to these,
Assyria, Babylon, Egypt, Idumea, and the like. In the former kind of allegory the primitive meaning is dropped, and
the figurative only is retained; in this, both the one and the
other are preserved, and this is what constitutes the difference.

"But of all the figures used by the prophets the most
frequent is the *metaphor*, by which words are transferred from
their primitive and plain to a secondary meaning. This
figure, common in all poetry and in all languages, is of in-
dispensable necessity in Scripture, which, having occasion
to speak of Divine and spiritual matters, could do it only
by terms borrowed from sensible and material objects. . . .
But though the prophets, partly from necessity and partly
from choice, are thus profuse in the use of metaphors, they
do not appear, like other writers, to have the liberty of using
them as fancy directed. The same set of images, however
diversified in the manner of applying them, is always used,
both in allegory and metaphor, to denote the same subjects,
to which they are in a manner appropriated. This peculiar
characteristic of the Hebrew poetry might perhaps be owing
to some rules taught in the prophetic schools, which did not
allow the same latitude in this respect as other poetry. Whatever it may be owing to, the uniform manner in which the
prophets apply these images tends greatly to illustrate the
prophetic style; and therefore it will be proper now to consider the *sources* from which those images are most frequently
derived, and the *subjects* and *ideas* which they severally
denote. These sources may be classed under four heads;

natural, artificial, religious, and *historical.* [Note: Unless otherwise noted, quotations below are from Isaiah.]

"I. The first and most copious, as well as the most pleasing source of images in the prophetic writings, as in all other poetry, is *nature;* and the principal images drawn. from nature, together with their application, are the following: —

"The *sun, moon,* and *stars,* the highest objects in the natural world, figuratively represent *kings, queens,* and *princes* or *rulers;* the highest in the world politic. . . .

"*Light* and *darkness* are used figuratively for *joy* and *sorrow,* prosperity and adversity. 'We wait for *light,* but behold *obscurity;* for *brightness,* but we walk in *darkness;*' chap. lix. 9. An uncommon degree of light denotes an uncommon degree of joy and prosperity, and *vice versa.* 'The light of the *moon* shall be as the light of the *sun,* and the light of the sun shall be *sevenfold;*' chap. xxx. 26. The same metaphors are likewise used to denote *knowledge* and *ignorance.* 'If they speak not according to this word, it is because there is no *light* in them;' chap. viii. 20. 'The people that walked in darkness have seen a great *light;*' chap. ix. 2.

"*Dew, moderate rains, gentle streams,* and *running waters* denote the *blessings of the Gospel.* 'Thy *dew* is as the dew of herbs;' chap. xxvi. 19. 'He shall come unto us as the rain;' Hosea vi. 3. 'I will *water* it every moment;' chap. xxvii. 3. 'I will pour *water* on him that is thirsty;' chap. xliv. 3.

"*Immoderate rains* on the other hand, *hail, floods, deep waters, torrents,* and *inundations,* denote *judgments* and *destruction.* 'I will rain upon him an *overflowing rain,* and *great hailstones,*' Ezek. xxxviii. 22. 'Waters rise up out of the north, and shall overflow the land,' Jer. xlvii. 2.

"*Fire* also, and the *east wind,* parching and hurtful, frequently denote the same. 'They shall cast thy choice cedars into the *fire,*' Jer. xxii. 7. 'He stayeth his *rough wind* in the day of the *east wind,*' Isa. xxvii. 8.

"*Wind* in general is often taken in the same sense. 'The *wind* shall eat up all thy pastures,' Jer. xxii. 22. Sometimes it is put for any thing *empty* or *fallacious,* as well as hurtful.

'The prophets shall become *wind*,' Jer. v. 13. 'They have sown the *wind*, and they shall reap the *whirlwind*,' Hos. viii. 7.

"*Lebanon* and *Carmel*; the one remarkable for its *height* and stately *cedars*, was the image of *majesty, strength*, or anything very *great* or *noble*. 'He shall cut down the thickets of the *forest* with iron, and *Lebanon* shall fall by a mighty one,' Isa. x. 34. 'The Assyrian was a *cedar* in Lebanon,' Ezek. xxxi. 3. The other mountain (*Carmel*) being fruitful, and abounding in vines and olives, denoted *beauty* and *fertility*. 'The glory of Lebanon shall be given it, the excellency of *Carmel*,' Isa. xxxv. 2. The vine alone is a frequent image of the Jewish Church. 'I had planted thee a noble *vine*,' Jer. ii. 21.

"*Rams* and *bullocks of Bashan, lions, eagles, sea-monsters*, or any *animals of prey*, are figures frequently used for cruel and oppressive *tyrants* and *conquerors*. 'Hear this word, ye *kine* of *Bashan*, which oppress the poor,' Amos iv. 1. 'The *lion* is come up from his thicket,' Jer. iv. 7. 'A great *eagle* came unto Lebanon, and took the *highest branch* of the cedar,' Ezek. xvii. 3. 'Thou art as a *whale* in the seas,' Ezek. xxxii. 2. 'The *unicorns* shall come down, and their land shall be soaked with blood,' Isa. xxxiv. 7.

"II. The ordinary *occupations* and *customs* of life, with the few *arts* practised at the time, were another source from which the prophets derived many of their figures, particularly,

"From *husbandry* in all its parts, and from its *implements*. 'Sow to yourselves in righteousness, reap in mercy: break up your fallow ground,' Hos. x. 12. 'Put in the *sickle*, for the harvest is ripe,' Joel iii. 13. 'I am pressed under you, as a *wain* under a load of sheaves,' Amos ii. 13. *Threshing* was performed in various ways, (mentioned Isa. xxviii. 24, &c.,) which furnish a variety of images denoting punishment. 'Arise and thresh, O daughter of Zion; for I will make thine *horn* iron, and thy *hoofs* brass,' &c., Micah iv. 13. The operation was performed on rising grounds, where the *chaff* was driven away by the wind, while the *grain* remained; a fit

emblem of the *fate of the wicked*, and of the *salvation of the just*.
'Behold, I will make thee a new *threshing-instrument* having
teeth; thou shalt thresh the mountains, and beat them small,
and thou shalt make the hills as *chaff*. Thou shalt *fan* them,
and the wind shall carry them away, and the *whirlwind* shall
scatter them,' Isa. xli. 15, 16.

"The *vintage* and *winepress* also furnish many images,
obvious enough in their application. 'The *press* is full, the
fats overflow, for their wickedness is great,' Joel iii. 13. 'I
have trod the *winepress* alone. I will tread down the people
in mine anger,' Isa. lxiii. 3, &c. As the *vintage* was gathered
with *shouting* and *rejoicing*, the ceasing of the vintage-shouting
is frequently one of the figures that denote *misery* and *deso-
lation*. 'None shall *tread* with *shouting;* their *shouting* shall be
no *shouting*,' Jer. xlviii. 33.

"From the occupation of *tending cattle* we have many
images. 'Wo unto the *pastors* that destroy and scatter the
sheep of my pasture,' Jer. xxiii. 1. The people are the *flock;*
teachers and *rulers* the *pastors*. 'Israel is a *scattered sheep*, the
lions have driven him away.' 'As a *shepherd* taketh out of the
mouth of the lion two legs, or a piece of an ear,' &c., Amos
iii. 12. Some of the images derived from *husbandry, tending
cattle*, &c., may perhaps appear mean to us; though not to
the Jews, whose manner of life was simple and plain, and
whose greatest men (such as Moses, David, Gideon, &c.)
were often *husbandmen* and *shepherds*. Accordingly, the
Messiah himself is frequently described under the character
of a *shepherd*. [See *Fleury's* Manners of the Israelites.]

"It was customary in deep mournings to *shave* the *head* and
beard, to retire to the *housetops*, which in those countries were
flat, and furnished with little chambers adapted to the purposes of devotion or of sequestered grief; also to sing dirges
at funerals, and to accompany them with a mournful sort
of music; and from these and the like circumstances images
are frequently borrowed by the prophets to denote the
greatest danger, and the *deepest distress*. 'Mine heart shall sound
for Moab like pipes.' 'Every head shall be *bald*, and every

beard clipt—there shall be lamentation on all the *house-tops* of Moab,' Jer. xlviii. 36-38; Isa. xv. 2, 3. . . .

"According to the barbarous custom of those times, conquerors *drove their captives before them* almost *naked*, and exposed to the intolerable heat of the sun, and the inclemencies of the weather. They afterwards employed them frequently in *grinding at the handmill*, (watermills not being then invented;) hence *nakedness*, and *grinding at the mill*, and *sitting on the ground* (the posture in which they wrought) express captivity. 'Descend and sit in the dust, O virgin daughter of Babylon; take the *millstones*—thy *nakedness* shall be uncovered,' Isa. xlvii. 1-3.

"The *marriage relation* supplied metaphors to express the relation or covenant between God and his people. On the other hand *adultery, infidelity* to the *marriage bed,* &c., denoted any breach of covenant with God, particularly the *love and worship of idols*. 'Turn, O backsliding children, saith the Lord, for I am married unto you,' Jer. iii. 14. 'There were two women, the daughters of one mother, and they committed whoredoms—with their idols have they committed adultery,' &c., Ezek. xxiii. 2-37.

In this case, Israel was the mother, and Judah and Ephraim (Ephraim being a name for the Northern Kingdom, commonly called Israel after Israel split in two) were the two harlot daughters. Both Judah and Israel were untrue to their God, Jehovah, and went after the heathen gods of their neighbors.

"The *debility* and *stupefaction* caused by *intoxicating liquors* suggested very apt images to express the terrible effects of the Divine judgments on those who are the unhappy objects of them. 'Thou shalt be filled with drunkenness, with the cup of thy sister Samaria,' Ezek. xxiii. 33.

Latter-day Saints sometimes mistakenly think that this drunkenness has reference to breaking the Word of Wisdom. Actually it has reference to idolatry, as a careful examination of the above passage from Ezekiel shows. Samaria refers to the kingdom of Israel, which first abandoned itself to idolatry and was, therefore, carried away into captivity. This was before Ezekiel's day. He is saying that Judah, to whom he was a prophet, was about to partake of the same fate.

"From the method of *refining metals in the furnace* images are often borrowed to denote the *judgments* inflicted by God on his people, with a view to cleanse them from their sins, as metal from its dross. 'Israel is dross in the midst of the furnace,' Ezek. xxii. 18. 'He shall sit as a refiner and purifier of silver,' Mal. iii. 3.

"Among the other few arts from which the Hebrew poets derive some of their images, are those of the *fuller* and *potter*, Mal. iii. 2, &c.; Jer. xviii. 1, &c.; of which the application is obvious. No less so is that of images derived from *fishing, fowling,* and the *implements* belonging to them; the *hook, net, pit, snare,* &c., which generally denote *captivity* or *destruction.* . . . 'I will put hooks to thy jaws,' Ezek. xxix. 4. 'Fear, and the pit, and the snare, are upon thee, O inhabitant of the earth,' Isa. xxiv. 17.

"A few images are derived from *building,* as when the Messiah is denoted by a *foundation* and *corner-stone,* Isa. xxviii. 16. The next verse describes the *rectitude* of *judgment* by metaphors borrowed from the *line* and *plummet;* and by *building with precious stones* is denoted a very high degree of *prosperity,* whether applied to church or state, Isa. liv. 11, 12.

"III. Religion, and things connected with it, furnished many images to the sacred poets.

"From the *temple* and its pompous service, from the *tabernacle, shechinah, mercy-seat,* &c., are derived a variety of images, chiefly serving to denote the glory of the Christian Church, the excellency of its worship, God's favour towards it, and his constant presence with it; the prophets speaking to the Jews in terms accommodated to their own ideas. 'And the Lord will create upon every dwelling-place of Mount Zion, and upon her assemblies, a cloud and smoke by day, and the shining of a flaming fire by night; for upon all the glory shall be a covering,' Isa. iv. 5. 'Then will I sprinkle clean water upon you, and ye shall be clean,' Ezek. xxxvi. 25.

The *Shekhinah*, as it is spelled in current Jewish literature, is the glory or glorious presence of God. *Shekhinah* is the Jewish name of the holy light that shone from the holy place in the tabernacle during the sojourn in the wilderness. Quite rightly we might refer to it as the light that appeared around the Father and the Son in the Sacred Grove and that accompanied the angel Moroni when he appeared to Joseph Smith. More often than not Dr. Smith and Adam Clarke apply images to the Christian Church of Jesus' and the apostles' day that should be applied to The Church of Jesus Christ of Latter-day Saints. They also do not recognize that Zion refers to America and the city Zion, instead of to Jerusalem and the Mt. Zion of that city. So the reader must make allowances for these problems when he reads these commentaries.

"The *ceremonial law*, and especially its distinctions between things *clean* and *unclean*, furnished a number of images, all obvious in their application. 'Wash ye, make you clean, put away the evil of your doings,' Isa. i. 16. 'Their way was before me as the uncleanness of a removed woman,' Ezek. xxxvi. 17.

"The *killing of sacrifices* and *feasting upon them*, serve as metaphors for *slaughter*. 'The Lord hath a sacrifice in Bozrah,' Isa. xxxiv. 6; Ezek. xxxix. 17.

"The *pontifical robes*, which were very splendid, suggested several images expressive of the *glory* of both the Jewish and Christian Church. 'I clothed thee with broidered work,' &c., Ezek. xvi. 10. 'He clothed me with the garments of salvation,' Isa. lxi. 10. The prophets wore a *rough upper garment;* false prophets wore the like, in imitation of true ones; and to this there are frequent allusions. 'Neither shall they wear a rough garment to deceive,' Zech. xiii. 4.

"From the *pots,* and other *vessels* and *utensils* of the temple, are likewise borrowed a few metaphors obvious enough without explanation: 'Every pot in Jerusalem and in Judah shall be holiness,' Zech. xiv. 21.

"The prophets have likewise many images that allude to the *idolatrous rites* of the neighbouring nations, to their *groves* and *high places*, Isa. xxvii. 9, and to the worship paid to their idols, *Baal, Molech, Chemosh, Gad, Meni, Ashtaroth, Tammuz,* &c., Ezek. viii. 10-14.

"IV. Many of the metaphors and images used by the prophets are likewise borrowed from *history*, especially sacred.

"From the *fall of angels:* 'How art thou fallen from heaven, O Lucifer, son of the morning;' Isa. xiv. 12. 'Thou art the anointed cherub, — thou wast upon the holy mountain of God;' Ezek. xxviii. 14. And from *the fall of man:* 'Thou hast been in Eden, the garden of God;' ver. 13.

"From *chaos:* 'I beheld the earth, and, lo! it was without form, and void; and the heavens, and they had no light;' Jer. iv. 23. 'He shall stretch over it the line of devastation, and the plummet of emptiness;' Isa. xxxiv. 11.

"From the *deluge:* 'The windows from on high are open, and the foundations of the earth do shake;' Isa. xxiv. 18.

"From the *destruction of Sodom and Gomorrah:* 'And the streams thereof shall be turned into pitch, and the dust thereof into brimstone, and the land thereof shall become burning pitch;' Isa. xxxiv. 9. Also from the destruction of the Hivites and Amorites, &c., Isa. xvii. 9.

"The *exodus* and *deliverance from Egypt,* is frequently used to shadow forth other great deliverances: 'Thus saith the Lord, who maketh a way in the sea, and a path in the mighty waters,' &c.; Isa. xi. 15, 16; xliii. 16-19; li. 9, 10, &c.

"From the *descent on Sinai:* 'Behold, the Lord cometh forth out of his place, and will come down and tread on the high places of the earth; and the mountains shall be molten under him;' Micah i. 3, 4. . . .

"The foregoing account of the images which most frequently occur in the writings of the prophets may be of considerable use in studying their style; but as a thorough knowledge of this must be allowed to be of the highest importance, a few *general remarks* are farther added, although some part of them may appear to be superseded by what has been already observed.

"1. Although the prophets use words so frequently in a figurative or metaphorical meaning; yet we ought not, without necessity, to depart from the primitive and original sense of language; and such a necessity there is, when the plain and original sense is less proper, less suitable to the subject and context, or contrary to other scriptures.

"2. By images borrowed from the world natural the prophets frequently understand something analogous in the world politic. Thus, the *sun, moon, stars,* and *heavenly bodies* denote *kings, queens, rulers,* and *persons* in *great power;* their *increase of splendour* denotes *increase of prosperity;* their *darkening, setting,* or *falling* denotes a *reverse of fortune,* or the entire ceasing of that power or kingdom to which they refer. *Great earthquakes,* and the *shaking of heaven and earth,* denote the *commotion* and *overthrow of kingdoms;* and the *beginning* or *end of the world,* their *rise* or *ruin.*

"3. The *cedars of Lebanon, oaks of Bashan, fir-trees,* and other *stately* trees of the forest, denote *kings, princes, potentates,* and *persons of the highest rank; briers* and *thorns,* the *common people,* or those of the meanest order.

"4. *High mountains* and *lofty hills,* in like manner, denote *kingdoms, republics, states,* and *cities; towers* and *fortresses* signify *defenders* and *protectors; ships of Tarshish,* merchants or commercial people; and the *daughter* of any capital or mother city, the *lesser cities* or *suburbs* around it. *Cities never conquered* are farther styled *virgins.*

"5. The prophets likewise describe *kings* and *kingdoms* by their *ensigns;* as *Cyrus* and the *Romans* by an *eagle,* the *king of Macedon* by a *goat,* and the *king of Persia* by a *ram;* these being the figures on their respective standards, or in the ornaments of their architecture.

"6. The prophets in like manner borrow some of their images from *ancient hieroglyphics,* which they take in their usual acceptation: thus, a *star* was the emblem of a *god* or *hero;* a *horn,* the emblem of *great power* or *strength;* and a *rod,* the emblem of *royalty;* and they signify the same in the prophets.

"7. The same prophecies have frequently a *double meaning;* and refer to different events, the one *near,* the other *remote;* the one *temporal,* the other *spiritual,* or perhaps *eternal.* The prophets having thus several events in their eye, their expressions may be partly applicable to one, and partly to another; and it is not always easy to mark the transitions. Thus, the prophecies relating to the *first* and *second restoration* of the *Jews,* and *first* and *second coming of our Lord,* are often interwoven together; like our Saviour's own prediction (Matt. xxiv.) concerning the *destruction of Jerusalem* and the *end of the world.* What has not been fulfilled in the first, we must apply to the second; and what has been already fulfilled may often be considered as typical of what still remains to be accomplished.

"8. We must not, however, expect to find always a mystical meaning in prophecy; and when the near and most obvious meaning is plain, and gives a good sense, we need not depart from it, nor be over-curious to look beyond it.

"9. In prophecies, as in parables, we are chiefly to consider the *scope* and *design,* without attempting too minute an explication of all the poetical images and figures which the sacred writers use to adorn their style.

"10. Prophecies of a general nature are applicable *by accommodation* to individuals; most of the things that are spoken of the Church in general being no less applicable to its individual members.

"11. Prophecies of a particular nature, on the other hand, admit, and often require, to be extended. Thus, Edom, Moab, or any of the enemies of God's people, is often put for the whole; what is said of one being generally applicable to the rest.

"12. In like manner, what is said to or of any of God's people, on any particular occasion, is of general application and use; all that stand in the same relation to God having an interest in the same promises.

"13. A *cup of intoxicating liquor* is frequently used to denote the *indignation of God;* and the effects of such a cup, the effects of his displeasure.

"14. As the *covenant of God* with his people is represented under the figure of *marriage;* so their *breach of that covenant,* especially their idolatry, is represented by *whoredom, adultery,* and *infidelity to the marriage bed;* on which the prophets sometimes enlarge, to excite detestation of the crime. The epithet *strange* does likewise, almost always, relate to something connected with *idolatry.*

"15. Persons or nations are frequently said in Scripture to be related to those whom they resemble in their life and conduct. In the same manner, men are denoted by *animals* whose qualities they resemble. A definite number, such as *three, four, seven, ten,* &c., is sometimes used by the prophets for an *indefinite,* and commonly denotes a *great many.*

"16. In the reckoning of time, a *day* is used by the prophets to denote a *year*; and things *still future,* to denote their certainty, are spoken of as *already past.* . . .

"18. When places are mentioned as lying *north, south, east,* or *west,* it is generally to be understood of their situation with respect to *Judea* or *Jerusalem,* when the context does not plainly restrict the scene to some other place.

"19. By the *earth,* or the word so translated, the prophets frequently mean the *land of Judea;* and sometimes, says Sir Isaac Newton, the great continent of all Asia and Africa, to which they had access by land. By the *isles of the sea,* on the other hand, they understood the places to which they sailed, particularly all Europe, and probably the islands and seacoasts of the Mediterranean.

It is not commonly known that Sir Isaac Newton was a great Bible scholar. The Book of Mormon implies that the continents of America also were "isles of the sea." See, for example 2 Nephi 10:20.

"20. The greatest part of the prophetic writings was first composed in *verse*, and still retains, notwithstanding all the disadvantages of a literal prose translation, much of the air and cast of the original, particularly in the division of the lines, and in that peculiarity of Hebrew poetry by which the sense of one line or couplet so frequently corresponds with that of the other. Thus:—

> I will greatly rejoice in the Lord,
> My soul shall be joyful in my God;
> For he hath clothed me with the garments of salvation,
> He hath covered me with the robe of righteousness:
> As a bridegroom decketh himself with ornaments,
> And as a bride adorneth herself with her jewels.
>
> Isa. lxi. 10

"Attention to this peculiarity in sacred poetry will frequently lead to the meaning of many passages in the poetical parts of Scripture, in which it perpetually occurs, as the one line of a couplet, or member of a sentence, is generally a commentary on the other. Thus:—

> The Lord hath a sacrifice in Bozrah,
> And a great slaughter in the land of Idumea.
>
> Isa. xxxiv. 6.

"Here the metaphor in the first line is expressed in plain terms in the next: the *sacrifice in Bozrah* means the *great slaughter in Idumea*, of which Bozrah was the capital.

"It must be observed that the *parallelism* is frequently more extended. Thus:—

> For I will pour out waters on the thirsty,
> And flowing streams upon the dry ground;

> I will pour out my Spirit on thy seed,
> And my blessing on thine offspring.
>
> Isa. xliv. 3

"Here the two last lines explain the metaphor in the two preceding." (Clarke, 4:7-13.)

It would take a commentary of several thousand pages to fully explore all of the figurative devices alluded to above, but a few more fully developed illustrations may be helpful.

The use of dual or multiple meanings can be illustrated by Psalm 69:20-21. In fact, the whole context could very well be applicable. It was an essential characteristic of the Psalms to address the Lord or put words in his mouth that could be accepted as authoritative. Hence, often (if not always) a psalm would carry a double meaning. David, for example, would be the speaker and he would indeed be speaking of some real trial that he had been through (such as his exile from Saul or during Absalom's insurrection) in which he may have eaten liver that was not free from gall and may have drunk wine that was vinegary or sour, and then he would say, "They gave me also gall for my meat; and in my thirst they gave me vinegar to drink." (Psalm 69:21.) Perhaps he had learned by revelation or from scriptures then in existence that this would happen to Jesus while on the cross. (See Matthew 27:34.) Or he may have had some plain and precious revelation about Jesus that has since been lost, and this revelation—or earlier psalm—may have told him of Jesus' experience on the cross. And, in the agony of his exile and betrayal, and in the great inconvenience of eating inferior food and drinking inferior wine, he may have composed these words that likened his suffering to that of Jesus. Thus he was laying his own case

before the Lord and man; and, at the same time, calling
attention to the suffering of our Redeemer on the cross.

It is said in the Jewish Targum that Psalm 91 is a
dialogue between David and Solomon, with the Lord interjecting statements here and there. Thus David may be the
speaker in verse 1; then Solomon responds in verse 2; David
then speaks from verses 3-13; and then the Lord gives his
blessing in verses 14-16. If this be the case, this psalm has
a dual meaning, because verses 11 and 12 are considered
messianic — that is, they refer to the Father's solicitude for
his Son, Jesus. (See Luke 4:10-11.)

The blessings which Jacob gave his twelve sons are full
of very difficult figurative language. Note how the following
commentary supports what the prophets have told us about
the blessing of Joseph:

> Vers. 22-26. Turning to Joseph, the patriarch's heart
> swelled with grateful love, and in the richest words and
> figures he implored the greatest abundance of blessings
> upon his head.
> Ver. 22. "*Son of a fruit-tree is Joseph, son of a fruit-tree at the
> well, daughters run over the wall.*" Joseph is compared to the
> branch of a fruit-tree planted by a well (Ps. i. 3), which
> sends its shoots over the wall, and by which, according to
> Ps. lxxx., we are probably to understand a vine. . . .
> Vers. 23, 24. "*Archers provoke him, and shoot and hate him;
> but his bow abides in strength, and the arms of his hands remain
> pliant, from the hands of the Mighty One of Jacob, from thence, from
> the Shepherd, the Stone of Israel.*" From the simile of the fruit-
> tree Jacob passed to a warlike figure, and described the
> mighty and victorious unfolding of the tribe of Joseph in
> conflict with all its foes, describing with prophetic intuition
> the future as already come (*vid.* the *perf. consec.*). The words
> are not to be referred to the personal history of Joseph him-
> self, to persecutions received by him from his brethren, or

to his sufferings in Egypt; still less to any warlike deeds of
his in Egypt (*Diestel*): they merely pointed to the conflicts
awaiting his descendants, in which they would constantly
overcome all hostile attacks.

. . . The words which follow, "from the hands of the
Mighty One of Jacob," are not to be linked to what follows,
in opposition to the Masoretic division of the verses; they
rather form one sentence with what precedes: "pliant remain the arms of his hands from the hands of God," *i.e.*
through the hands of God supporting them. "The Mighty
One of Jacob," He who had proved Himself to be the
Mighty One by the powerful defence afforded to Jacob; a
title which is copied from this passage in Isa. i. 24, etc.
"From thence," an emphatic reference to Him, from whom
all perfection comes—"from the Shepherd (xlviii. 15) and
Stone of Israel." God is called "the Stone," and elsewhere
"the Rock" (Deut. xxxii. 4, 18, etc.), as the immoveable
foundation upon which Israel might trust, might stand firm
and impregnably secure.

Vers. 25, 26. "*From the God of thy father, may He help thee,
and with the help of the Almighty, may He bless thee,* (may there
come) *blessings of heaven from above, blessings of the deep, that
lieth beneath, blessings of the breast and of the womb. The blessing
of thy father surpass the blessings of my progenitors to the border of
the everlasting hills, may they come upon the head of Joseph, and
upon the crown of the illustrious among his brethren.*" From the
form of a description the blessing passes in ver. 25 into the
form of a desire, in which the "from" of the previous clause
is still retained. The words "and may He help thee," "may
He bless thee," form parentheses, for "who will help and
bless thee." (*Commentary on the Old Testament*, 1:406-07.)

ASSUMING THAT MOSES, ISAIAH AND ALL THE PROPHETS WERE "MORMONS"

When many of the scholars of the world read the Old
Testament they think of the people portrayed there as Jews,

which is correct enough except that they tend to think of Jews as non-Christians or anti-Christians. And some are so obsessed with the idea that they think of the Jews of Jesus' day as more advanced than the Jews or Israelites of Moses' day. This is a fallacy. The Israelites of Moses' day were far ahead of the Jews of Jesus' day in government, in law, in philosophy and practice of economic law, in social relations and in religion. From Moses' day onward there was a constant regression in religion and social well-being. In fact, this regression commenced much earlier than Moses' day. Abraham and his descendants down to Joseph's day, perhaps a little later, had the fulness of the gospel. By Moses' time the Israelites had fallen a long way. Most scholars think they partook deeply of the idolatry of the Egyptians. So, in that sense, the law of Moses was a great lift upward for them. But then the descent began again. Of course, the *Christians* of Jesus' day were Jews who were ahead of those of Moses' day. But the dispensation of Jesus did not last long. And then both Christian Jews and those who still claimed to follow Moses regressed even more rapidly for hundreds of years.

After Jesus had come and had been rejected, the Jews became non-Christian and anti-Christian. Then the central figure of earlier Judaism, the Messiah, lost significance, even though there are still some who look for a Messiah and for Elijah's return. Then all the outward things—the peculiar dress, the formal celebrations, and the legalities which started with Moses and were embellished after the Captivity (embellishments which Jesus had noted with disapproval)—became everything. Often this apostate Jew is the Jew that the scholars visualize when they read the Old Testament. This is not a helpful pattern; it does not increase understanding of the writings of the prophets. One must think of Isaiah, for example, as a very knowledgeable Latter-day Saint—perhaps as an apostle, or, more likely, as the president and prophet of the Church. Of course, the Church was organized differently under the law of Moses. But Isaiah was of the spiritual stature of a modern Church president, even though the office was not precisely the same in its title and jurisdiction.

And we should think of the Israelites in general as members of the true Church of Christ. True, they had a lesser law, but their religious knowledge was not contradictory or antithetical to ours. And those who best observed the law were probably equal in righteousness and spiritual knowledge to those who best keep the commandments today. We must think of Moses, Isaiah, Ezekiel, etc., as the best, all of whom received personal visitations from Jesus, whom they called Jehovah, the God of Israel, the Son of Man, the Son of Righteousness, and other titles that we still use today in the restored Church.

By assuming that they were true Christians, we will begin to understand many passages that would otherwise have no meaning. For example, Isaiah 53 is a beautiful prophecy of Jesus that gives many details of his life. Abinadi explained it and put it in proper perspective in Mosiah 14-16. The Jews go to great lengths to make this chapter (53) of Isaiah into an allegory, stating that the suffering servant is the Jewish nation, not Jesus.

Another passage that is enriched by our knowledge that the ancient Jews knew about Jesus, that he was Jehovah, their Savior and God, is Psalm 22.

The book of Job also takes on greater meaning to a Latter-day Saint. The world describes it as a superb poetical essay on the meaning of suffering. And, of course, they are right as far as they can go. But a Latter-day Saint sees far more. Not only a rich and primitive king of unusually good character, Job was also a patriarch in one of the lines of Abraham. No doubt he had been endowed, and had had his family sealed to him for eternity, and he knew about the premortal and postmortal worlds. That is why he was so family-oriented and so concerned about not having his wife given to another and his posterity rooted out. It explains why, when everything else was doubled, his second family was the same size as the first—because, of course, he still had the first. Therefore, his family was doubled, too. Many of Job's most passionate pleas would have no meaning, or a different meaning, if he had not been a king and a priest to the Most High God.

With this approach to Job we begin to see that the Lord was forcing Job to come to him and receive the Second Comforter. With his wealth, his great faith, his satisfaction to be busy helping others, Job was content—busy, yes; but content. He would not have sought the ultimate mortal experience if he had not been pushed to it. His suffering caused him to plead for an audience with the Heavenly King so that he could demand an explanation for what he felt was unjust treatment. When he was sufficiently humbled and refined, he got his audience. But then he no longer wanted to plead his case, saying: "I have heard of thee by the hearing of the ear: but now mine eye seeth thee. Wherefore I abhor myself, and repent in dust and ashes." (Job 42:5-6.) To a Latter-day Saint who accepts Job as a "Former-day Saint," that statement is not the literary style of the world's greatest poet—for the world concedes that the

writer of Job was the world's greatest poet. But it is the
testimony of a prophet who actually saw God as he really is.

Had he not been pushed to it, Job would not have
seen God and the book of Job would not have been written.
And its value is beyond any human calculation. It was part
of the Lord's plan for the mortal world to follow. The
eternal perspective that only Latter-day Saints have is
necessary to understand Job and the value of the book of
Job. It is, of course, valuable to the world, even if they do
not fully understand it. But the Latter-day Saint should be
able to see more. He sees in it the doctrine of witnesses of
God. He sees the price that has to be paid for the greatest
spiritual experiences. He sees words and phrases that only
a temple-going Latter-day Saint would see.

There are, of course, limits to how far we can push this
concept of assuming that Moses, Isaiah, and other prophets
were "Mormons." They were true Christians. Their names
are in the same Lamb's book of life that contains the
names of the Saints of our dispensation. The basic theology
is the same in all dispensations, though there are cultural
differences. The Jews were affected somewhat by their
environment just as we are, only their environment was
different. Their nation was often more homogenous in
culture and religion. They generally had only one official
religion, even when they mixed it with pagan idolatry.
Hence, many of their religious laws were also civil laws.
They were not particularly opposed to the union of church
and state; and, when all were of the same religion, it was
not uncommon to have priests and prophets wielding great
influence in and on government. There is little evidence
that this was considered bad; what was considered bad was a

situation in which conquerors imposed their pagan state religions upon the Jews and took their children under the wing of the state.

But whatever the cultural differences between modern and ancient Saints, faithful Latter-day Saints should feel very comfortable with the Old Testament. Such gospel principles as honesty, integrity, personal responsibility, and a caring attitude are constantly inculcated, from the Ten Commandments in Exodus to the book of Malachi. In today's climate of heavy taxation, too, we note that the Old Testament is a testimony of the evils of big and powerful governments that encroach upon private property rights. One of David's great virtues was the general absence of compulsory taxes and bureaucracy in his kingdom. Solomon introduced both with a vengeance, and, in doing so, fulfilled the dire predictions of Moses (see Deuteronomy 28:36) and of Samuel (1 Samuel 8:6-18; 12:1-25), and put Israel and Judah into the grasp of wicked kings.

OLD TESTAMENT PROPHETS BELIEVED SAME PLAN OF DOCTRINE WE BELIEVE

Nearly everyone who reads the Bible has an overall philosophy or explanation of life. This is sometimes called a world picture, or what members of the Church call the "plan of salvation"—where we come from, why we are here and where we are going. It includes what we believe about the nature of God, the spirit world, and the universe in general. As a rule, more intelligent people are more concerned with the refinement of this world picture, as well as being less able to tolerate not having the answers. The kind of people who seriously read the Bible do have well-developed world pictures. And this world picture very often determines how the reader will interpret what he reads.

For example, in Ecclesiastes 9:10, the writer says ". . . there is no work, nor device, nor knowledge, nor wisdom in the grave, whither thou goest." The Jehovah's Witnesses and Seventh-day Adventists, for example, whose world picture denies the existence of spirits and of a spirit world, believe that this passage proves conclusively that they are right. Latter-day Saints find in this passage only a statement about the mortal body and the need of making the most of this life. If this were the only passage bearing on the existence or nonexistence of a spirit world, those who deny such existence might sustain their case; but the fact is there are many passages which tell of or imply the existence of the spirit world. Those who do not accept this explain away most of these passages; but the task of making the passages fit the particular denomination's world picture requires a great deal of wresting and twisting.

Reference was earlier made to Job 42:5, in which Job bore witness of his visual perception of the Lord. To a Latter-day Saint, this is a simple, straightforward testimony, because our world picture includes corporeal beings who are members of the Godhead. Even the personage of the Holy Ghost has substance, though it is too fine to be felt by mortal hands. But the orthodox Catholic and Protestant world pictures do not allow for a corporeal being of any kind in the spirit world, let alone a corporeal deity. Therefore, they must have an explanation whenever the Lord appears. Dr. Adam Clarke, whose commentary agrees with us on an amazing number of Old Testament interpretations, nevertheless gave a typical anti-Christ twist to this passage. (See 1 John 4:1-2 for an explanation of an anti-Christ.) He paraphrased Job's testimony as follows: "I have now such a discovery of thee as I have never had before. I have only heard of thee by tradition, or from imperfect information; now the eye of my mind clearly perceives thee; and in seeing thee, I see myself; for the light that discovers thy glory and excellence, discovers my meanness and vileness." (Clarke, 3:191-92.)

One would have to be quite conversant with Dr. Clarke to appreciate the full significance of the above commentary. Suffice it to say that this statement was designed to give his fellow Christian ministers a way to wrest this simple and straightforward testimony of Job's eyewitness experience into something completely allegorical.

Also, Dr. Clarke ridiculed the idea that Isaiah 14:12-20 could refer to Satan. He said, "And although the context speaks explicitly concerning Nebuchadnezzar, yet this has been, I know not why, applied to the chief of the fallen angels, who is most incongruously denominated *Lucifer* (the bringer of light!), an epithet as common to him as those of *Satan* and *Devil*. That the Holy Spirit by his prophets should call this arch-enemy of God and man the *light-bringer*, would be strange indeed." (Clarke, 4:82.)

Of course, Adam Clarke is correct in his assertion that the passage refers to King Nebuchadnezzar. But it also refers to Satan—which is what gives meaning to the passage. Nebuchadnezzar's fall was being compared to a well-known premortal spirit world event—the fall of a son of the morning. We know this because this event is very important to our understanding of our world picture or plan of salvation. We have learned that a third of our Heavenly Father's premortal spirit family rebelled and were "cast out into the earth" (Revelation 12:9). In the "orthodox" world picture of medieval Christianity, which Adam Clarke would have inherited, the devils and angels were creations of God, not his children. None of them come to earth to obtain bodies, and they assume all sorts of forms. The devils are fallen angels—for the Lord did not create any as devils to begin with. Dr. Clarke's rejection of this passage as a reference to Lucifer came from his beliefs about devils. But we would not be able to support our interpretation of it any better than Clarke does his if it were not for modern revelation about the premortal spirit world. (See Abraham 3:27-28.)

It is a great testimony to a Latter-day Saint to read the Old Testament and discover again and again that something shows up that only a Latter-day Saint will see, let alone believe. From Adam to Malachi the prophets bear witness of the same doctrines we cherish.

OLD TESTAMENT UNDERSTOOD BY SPIRIT OF PROPHECY

After Paul was converted he became painfully aware that, because he had fallen into the same trap into which most Jews had fallen, he had not understood the Old Testament at all. The Jews were "looking beyond the mark" (Jacob 4:14). This mark was Jesus, and they looked beyond him to the laws and rituals that the Lord had given them (and those they had devised themselves) to teach them to look for Christ. Paul implied that Israel was afflicted by the Lord with a blindness of spirit that would persist until the time of the "fulness of the Gentiles" has arrived (Romans 11:25). On several occasions Paul quoted Isaiah 6:9-10 and applied it to the Jews of his day. When he was under house arrest in Rome, awaiting his trial, he called for the prominent Jews of the city to visit him. When they came, he "expounded and testified the kingdom of God, persuading them concerning Jesus, both out of the law of Moses, and out of the prophets, *from morning till evening.*" (Acts 28:23, emphasis added.) Paul indicated his understanding of Jesus in the Old Testament. Some believed him and some didn't. When they couldn't agree, they left, but not until Paul again had quoted Isaiah 6:9-10:

> . . . Well spake the Holy Ghost by Esaias the prophet unto our fathers,
>
> Saying, Go unto this people, and say, Hearing ye shall hear, and shall not understand; and seeing ye shall see, and not perceive:
>
> For the heart of this people is waxed gross, and their ears are dull of hearing, and their eyes have they closed; lest they should see with their eyes, and hear with their ears, and understand with their heart, and should be converted, and I should heal them.
>
> Be it known therefore unto you, that the salvation of God is sent unto the Gentiles, and that they will hear it.
>
> And when he had said these words, the Jews departed, and had great reasoning among themselves." (Acts 28:25-29.)

It is not "great reasoning" that opens the Old Testament; it is the light of the Spirit that comes after finding the Savior and being born again. That is partly why Jacob said that the first quest in life is to obtain a hope in Christ, or, in other words, find the kingdom of God. (See Jacob 2:18-19.)

"The testimony of Jesus is the spirit of prophecy." (Revelation 19:10.) For this reason Paul said that the gift of prophecy is more helpful to the Church than the gift of tongues or any other gift. (See 1 Corinthians 14:1-5.) Every prophet before Jesus foretold his coming. (See Jacob 7:11.)

One thing that we must remember about the spirit of prophecy (or the testimony of Jesus Christ) is that it grows as love of Christ and emulation of him grow. Another is that special prophets, seers, and revelators are called, set apart and sustained. Their commentary on the scriptures is the best, all things considered, that we can obtain.

Jesus, or Jehovah, the Savior, was uppermost in the mind of every prophet. The very fabric of their knowledge of Jesus was woven into their prophetic utterances. There would be no real meaning if this knowledge of Jesus was somehow unravelled from the mosaic of prophecy in the Old Testament. He was the bone onto which their words placed flesh. Thus, their knowledge of him shaped the whole body of Old Testament scripture. But the words of the prophets were a mystery to the spiritually blind. The words of Jacob in the Book of Mormon are very interesting in this regard:

> For, for this intent have we written these things, that they may know that we knew of Christ, and we had a hope of his glory many hundred years before his coming; and not only we ourselves had a hope of his glory, but also all the holy prophets which were before us.
>
> Behold, they believed in Christ and worshiped the Father in his name, and also we worship the Father in his name. And for this intent we keep the law of Moses, it pointing our souls to him; and for this cause it is sanctified unto us for righteousness, even as it was accounted unto Abraham in the wilderness to be obedient unto the commands of God in offering up his son Isaac, which is a similitude of God and his Only Begotten Son.
>
> Wherefore, we search the prophets, and we have many revelations and the spirit of prophecy; and having all these

witnesses we obtain a hope, and our faith becometh unshaken, insomuch that we truly can command in the name of Jesus and the very trees obey us, or the mountains, or the waves of the sea. . . .

But behold, the Jews were a stiffnecked people; and they despised the words of plainness, and killed the prophets, and sought for things that they could not understand. Wherefore, because of their blindness, which blindness came by looking beyond the mark, they must needs fall; for God hath taken away his plainness from them, and delivered unto them many things which they cannot understand, because they desired it. And because they desired it God hath done it, that they may stumble.

And now I, Jacob, am led on by the Spirit unto prophesying; for I perceive by the workings of the Spirit which is in me, that by the stumbling of the Jews they will reject the stone upon which they might build and have safe foundation.

But behold, according to the scriptures, this stone shall become the great, and the last, and the only sure foundation, upon which the Jews can build. (Jacob 4:4-6, 14-16.)

VALUE OF OLD TESTAMENT COMMENTARIES

In chapter one of this book considerable comments were made concerning the differences between the higher critic approach to the Old Testament and the more fundamental approach. This helps illustrate why the reader must exercise some caution and selectivity in the use of commentaries. For instance, even the best of sectarian Christian or Jewish commentaries have little value when commenting on theology; but they may have great value when commenting on history, languages and customs. Several examples have already been given showing how the commentaries misinterpret theology. Following are some examples of how they help in language, history, etc.

In Isaiah 44:2 we read, "Fear not, O Jacob, my servant; and thou, Jesurun, whom I have chosen." Clarke gives the following helpful explanation of the meaning of *Jesurun*:

> Verse 2. *Jesurun*] Jeshurun means Israel. This name was given to that people by Moses, Deut. xxxii. 15; xxxiii. 5, 26. The most probable account of it seems to be that in which the Jewish commentators agree; namely, that it is derived from *yashar*, and signifies *upright*. In the same manner, Israel, as a people, is called *meshullam, perfect*, [Ezra] chap. xiii. 19. They were taught of God, and abundantly furnished with the means of rectitude and perfection in his service and worship. Grotius thinks that *yeshurun* is a diminutive of *yishrael, Israel;* expressing peculiar fondness and affection; *O little Israel*. (Clarke, 4:173.)

In Isaiah 44:5, and elsewhere, reference is made to subscribing or inscribing with one's hand or inscribing one's hand to Jehovah. This alludes to an ancient form of tattooing the hand or some other part of a slave or employee to show the ownership of his master. Punctures were made and rendered indelible by fire or by staining. Soldiers were tattooed with the names of their commanders, and idolaters with the name of their gods. So this custom, as used in reference to believers, is a metaphor signifying the ownership of Jehovah. (Clarke, 4:174. Keil and Delitzsch reject this explanation on the grounds that Jewish law prohibited tattooing. But since it is only a metaphor that expresses the submission of the true Christian to becoming "clay in the Potter's hands," this is a weak reason for rejecting such an explanation. Of course, no Jew tattooed the name of Jehovah on his hand; but that name was written on the converted Jew's heart — figuratively speaking.)

There are many references to "high places" and "groves" in the Old Testament. (See, for example, 2 Kings 14:3-4.) In telling the history of the Hebrew kings, the chronicler would sometimes praise a certain king for his goodness, especially if he tore down the images and temples of the idolaters. But only rarely was a king so good that he tore down the "high places." In a number of passages this failure was noted by the statement that such-and-such a king did right in the sight of God, "save that the high places were not removed: the people sacrificed and burnt incense still on the high places." (2 Kings 15:4.)

A great deal has been said by commentators about these high places. They were places where sacrifices were made in secluded or high places on the mountains. The reasons why they were abhorrent to the Lord are (1), they usually originated with the earlier Canaanite idolaters, and were just taken over by the Israelites, and (2), the Israelites often used them to offer up sacrifices that otherwise might have been perfectly acceptable. So they constituted a compromise—a mingling of truth with error, a respect for places holy to idolaters and an excuse for not going to the temple to sacrifice properly. The groves were especially abhorrent because they were used for fertility rites and the practice of sexual perversions by official male and female harlots who were sustained by the state when idolatry was the official religion. And, even when the high places were set up only for the worship of Jehovah, the Lord did not approve, because sacrificing was to be done at the temple unless the Lord specified otherwise. Thus Asa was criticized mildly for not removing the "high places," even though his "heart was perfect with the Lord all his days." (1 Kings 15:14.) Note Clarke's comments:

Verse 14. *The high places were not removed*] He was not able
to make a thorough *reformation*; this was reserved for his son
Jehoshaphat.

   Asa's heart was perfect] He worshipped the true God, and
zealously promoted his service; see on ver. 3. And even the
high places which he did not remove were probably those
where the true God alone was worshipped; for that there
were such high places the preceding history amply proves,
and Jarchi intimates that these were places which individuals had erected for the worship of Jehovah. (Clarke,
2:446.)

See chapter five on the law of Moses for examples of
the value of commentaries on that sort of thing.

Another type of commentary that is valuable is one
which summarizes or draws together much or most of what
has been said on a particular subject. The value, of course,
depends on the accuracy and wisdom of the writer of the
commentary. One of the best examples of this type of commentary is Rousas John Rushdoony's *Institutes of Biblical
Law* (published by The Presbyterian and Reformed Publishing Company in 1973). This book uses the Ten Commandments and their expansion in the Bible, both Old and
New Testaments, as the framework for its discussion of
biblical law. It is an assumption of the author that the civil
code delivered by Moses must be distinguished from the
religious forms that were given by him as a lesser law. The
so-called law of Moses, the religion given in place of the
gospel, was done away in Christ. But the civil code never
was done away with. Rushdoony amply documents the fact
that it was the basis of all civil law of all Jewish and
Christian nations until the rise of humanism in quite recent
times. In fact, the civil code of Moses has not been totally
abrogated in the so-called Western nations.

In the following quotation from Rushdoony, he argues the biblical case against abortion:

> Abortion, the destruction of the human embryo or foetus, has long been regarded by Biblical standards as murder. The grounds for this judgment are the sixth commandment, and Exodus 21:22-25. Cassuto's "explanatory rendering" of this latter passage brings out its meaning: "When men strive together and they hurt unintentionally a woman with child, and her children come forth but no mischief happens —that is, the woman and the children do not die—the one who hurt her shall surely be punished by a fine. But if any mischief happens, that is, if the woman dies or the children die, then you shall give life for life." (Cited by John Warwick Montgomery in a letter to *Christianity Today*, vol. XIII, no. 5 [December 6, 1968], p. 28, from Cassuto, *Commentary on the Book of Exodus* [Jerusalem: Magnes Press, the Hebrew University, 1967].)
>
> The comment of Keil and Delitzsch is important: "If men strove and thrust against a woman with child, who had come near or between them for the purpose of making peace, so that her children come out (come into the world), and no injury was done either to the woman or the child that was born, a pecuniary compensation was to be paid, such as the husband of the woman laid upon him, and he was to give it . . . by (by an appeal to) arbitrators. A fine is imposed, because even if no injury had been done to the woman and the fruit of her womb, such a blow might have endangered life. . . . The plural . . . is employed for the purpose of speaking indefinitely, because there might possibly be more than one child in the womb. *'But if injury occur* (to the mother or the child), *thou shalt give soul for soul, eye for eye . . .* wound for wound': thus perfect retribution was to be made." (Keil and Delitzsch, *Pentateuch*, II, 134f.)
>
> It is interesting to note that antinomian dispensationalism [This is the philosophy of the radical "saved by grace" Christians and humanists which denies the need of obeying

law] sees no law here or elsewhere. Waltke of Dallas Theological Seminary sees no law against abortion here and, in
fact, feels that "abortion was permissible in the Old Testament law." (Bruce K. Waltke, "The Old Testament and
Birth Control," in *Christianity Today*, vol. XIII, no. 3 [No-
vember 8, 1968], p. 3 [99].)

The importance of Exodus 21:22-25 becomes all the more
clear as we realize that this is case law, i.e., that it sets forth
by a minimal case certain larger implications. Let us
examine some of the implications of this passage: *First,* very
obviously, the text cites, not a case of deliberate abortion
but a case of accidental abortion. If the penalty for even an
accidental case is so severe, it is obvious that a deliberately
induced abortion is very strongly forbidden. It is not necessary to ban deliberate abortion, since it is already eliminated
by this law. *Second,* the penalty for even an accidental abortion is death. If a man who, in the course of a fight, unintentionally bumps a pregnant woman and causes her to
abort, must suffer the death penalty, how much more so
any person who intentionally induces an abortion? *Third,*
even if no injury results to either the mother or the foetus,
the man in the case is liable to a fine and, in fact, must be
fined. Clearly, the law strongly protects the pregnant
woman and her foetus, so that every pregnant mother has
a strong hedge of law around her. *Fourth,* since even a
mother bird with eggs or young is covered by law (Deut.
22:6, 7), clearly any tampering with the fact of birth is a
serious matter: to destroy life is forbidden except where required or permitted by God's law. (*Institutes of Biblical Law*,
pages 263-64.)

Rushdoony follows the above quotation with several
pages that trace the history of the acceptance of abortion
and its foundations in the totalitarian state from antiquity
on down, in humanism and in apostate Christianity. On the
one hand we have God's law; on the other, the humanistic
law that is based in environmentalism.

In the following commentary, and also in his chapter on the sixth commandment, Rushdoony points out that there is no such thing as a neutral education. Our children receive either a Christian education or an anti-Christian education. Education must be presented from some point of view—in other words, from the foundations of one philosophy or another. Anything but a Christian philosophy will be an anti-Christian philosophy. Under the civil code that God gave through Moses, the greatest lawgiver of all time, parents were responsible for the education of their children. Now the state is responsible, and this gives children a statist education which is basically anti-Christian. Part of Rushdoony's explanation follows:

> The basic premise of the modern doctrine of toleration is that all religious and moral positions are equally true and equally false. In brief, this toleration rests on a radical relativism and humanism. There is no particular truth or moral value in any religion; the true value is man himself, and man as such must be given total acceptance, irrespective of his moral or religious position. Thus, Walt Whitman, in his poem, "To a Common Prostitute," declared, "Not till the sun excludes you, do I exclude you." *Total acceptance and total integration* are demanded by this relativistic humanism. Thus, this position, by reducing all non-humanistic positions to equality, and then setting man above them as lord, is radically antichristian. It places man in God's place and, in the name of toleration and equality, relegates Christianity to the junk-heap.
>
> But integration and equality are myths; they disguise a new segregation and a new inequality. "Mama Leone's" letter makes clear that, in her view, promiscuity is superior to virginity. This means a new segregation: virtue is subjected to hostility, scorn, and is separated for destruction.
>
> Every social order institutes its own program of separation or segregation. A particular faith and morality is given

privileged status and all else is separated for progressive elimination. The claim of equality and integration is thus a pretext to subvert an older or existing form of social order.

State control of education has been a central means of destroying Christian order. It excludes from the curriculum everything which points to the truth of Biblical faith and establishes a new doctrine of truth. In the name of objective reason, it insists that its highly selective hostility to Biblical faith be regarded as a law of being.

Education is a form of segregation, and, in fact, a basic instrument thereof as well. By means of education, certain aspects of life and experience are given the priority of truth and others are relegated to unimportance or are classed as wrong. Education inescapably segregates and classifies all reality in terms of certain premises or presuppositions. These premises are religious premises and are always pre-theoretical and are determinative of all thinking.

Not only education but law also segregates. Every law-order, by legislating against certain types of conduct, requires a segregation in terms of its premises. The segregation demanded by the democratic and the Marxist states is as radical and thorough as any history has seen, if not more so.

All religions segregate also, and humanism is certainly no exception. Every religion asserts an order of truth, and every other order is regarded as a lie. Humanism is relativistic with respect to all other religions, but it is absolutistic with respect to man. Man is the absolute of humanism, and all else is treated as error.

Segregation, separation, or quarantine, whichever name is used, is inescapable in any society. The radical libertarian claims that he will permit total liberty for all positions, i.e., a free market for all ideas and religions. But he outlaws all positions which deny his own. In the academic world these libertarians have proven to be ruthless enemies of Biblical faith, denying its right to a hearing. The state cannot exist, in such a libertarian order, nor can the church except on the enemy's terms. The new libertarians are congenial to Marxists, but not to Christians. While ostensibly against coercion, they are not above a common front with Marxists, as the libertarian journal *Left and Right* indicated. For the truth of Scripture, they have no toleration, nor any "common front" except a surrender on their terms. Every faith is an exclusive way of life; none is more dangerous than that which maintains the illusion of tolerance. An openly heartless faith is surely dangerous, but a heartless faith which believes in itself as a loving agent is even more to be feared.

Because no agreement is possible between truth and a lie, between heaven and hell, St. Paul declared, "Wherefore come out from among them, and be ye separate, saith the Lord, and touch not the unclean thing: and I will receive you" (II Cor. 6:17). [*Institutes of Biblical Law*, pages 295-97.]

Some may remember a newspaper account in the late sixties or early seventies of a woman being molested and murdered within the eyesight and earshot of dozens of people in New York City. While these people were fully aware of the crime—some even watched it—none of them came to the woman's rescue. This is not an isolated case.

In the civil code of Moses, such failure to rush to the rescue of a stricken person was a crime of great stature that demanded punishment. Rushdoony treats it in his chapter on the eighth commandment because it generally involves property loss and is related to being a party to a theft.

Failure to render aid was once a serious offense, and to a limited degree, still makes the man who fails to render aid liable to serious penalties. The direction of humanistic law is progressively absolving men of any legal obligation to be a Good Samaritan. Thus, according to one decision, "a bystander may watch a blind man or a child walk over a precipice, and yet he is not required to give warning. He may stand on the bank of a stream and see a man drowning, and although he holds in his hand a rope that could be used to rescue the man, yet he is not required to give assistance. He may owe a moral duty to warn the blind man or to assist the drowning man, but being a mere bystander, and in nowise responsible for the dangerous situation, he owes no legal duty to render assistance.'' (Bushanan v. Rose [1942] 128 Tex. 390, 159 Sw2d 109, 110 [Alexander, C.J.] cited in Clark: *Biblical Law*, p. 121.)

In certain cases, however, the bystander must render aid or face legal action. A bystander can watch a farmer's house or barn burn and do nothing, but in the case of a forest fire (federal ''property''), the bystander must render action as demanded or face penalties from a court.

Formerly, all bystanders had a legal duty to render aid to a *hue and cry*. The expression, *hue and cry*, is a legal term; formerly, when a criminal escaped, or was discovered, or an act of crime was being committed, the summons to assist was legally binding on all. Later, *hue and cry* was the name of a written proclamation asking for the apprehension of a criminal, or of stolen goods. In England, *Hue and Cry* was also the title of an official gazette publishing information on crimes and criminals.

Biblical law, however, asserts the liability of the bystander. Thus, Deuteronomy 22:1-4, declares ''Thou shalt not see thy brother's ox nor his sheep go astray, and hide thyself from them; thou shalt in any case bring them again unto thy brother.

''And if thy brother be not nigh unto thee, or if thou know him not, then thou shalt bring it unto thine own house, and it shall be with thee, until thy brother seek after it, and thou shalt restore it to him again.

''In like manner shalt thou do with his ass; and so shalt thou do with his raiment; and with all lost things of thy brother's, which he hath lost, and thou hast found, shalt thou do likewise: thou mayest not hide thyself.

''Thou shalt not see thy brother's ass or his ox fall down by the way, and hide thyself from them: thou shalt surely help him to lift them up again.''

Here again we have case law, giving a minimal case in order to illustrate a general principle. We cannot rob a man of his property by our neglect; we must act as good neighbors even to our enemies and to strangers. Lost or strayed animals, property, or clothing must be protected and held in ward with every public effort at immediate restoration.

If the bystander has an obligation to render aid "with all lost things" of another man, he has an even more pressing obligation to help rescue the man. Thus, this principle of responsibility appears in Deuteronomy 22:24. A woman assaulted in a city is presumed to have given consent if she does not raise a cry, the origin of the *hue and cry* [of] common law. At her cry, every man within sound of her voice has a duty to render immediate aid; failure to do so was regarded as a fearful abomination which polluted the land and, figuratively, darkened the sun. The horror felt at such an offense is reflected in the rabbinic tradition:

"Our Rabbis taught, on account of four things is the sun in eclipse: On Account of an Ab Beth din (the vice-president of the Sanhedrin) who died and was not mourned fittingly; on account of a betrothed maiden who cried out aloud in the city and there was none to save her; on account of sodomy, and on account of two brothers whose blood was shed at the same time. And on account of four things are the luminaries (the moon and the stars) in eclipse: On account of those who perpetrate forgeries, on account of those who give false witness; on account of those who rear small cattle in the land of Israel (Animals that cannot be prevented from ravaging the fields of others); and on account of those who cut down good trees." (Sukkah 29a; in Seder Mo'ed, *The Babylonian Talmud*, III, 130f.)

It is significant that this offense is rated as worse than giving false witness; the false witness misrepresents the truth; the non-interfering bystander becomes an accomplice to the crime by his refusal to render aid. Asaph said of those who were indifferent to the need to render aid, "When thou sawest a thief, then thou consentedst with him; and has been partaker with adulterers (Ps. 50:18)."

Quite properly, the marginal references cite Romans 1:32 and I Timothy 5:22. In the latter passage, those who consent to the hasty ordination of novices in the faith, or by their silence give consent, are "partakers of other men's sins." It is not unreasonable to assume that the penalty for the inactive bystander was like that of the false witness. The penalty of the crime applied to the false witness (Deut. 19:18, 19); the inactive bystander is also a kind of witness, and one who consents to the crime by his failure to act. The inactive bystander is thus an accomplice, an accessory to the crime, and liable to the penalty for the crime.

Solomon also called attention to the same crime in sharp and pointed words declaring,

If thou forbear to deliver them that are drawn unto death, and those that are ready to be slain;

If thou sayest, Behold, we know it not; doth not he that pondereth the heart consider it? and he that keepeth thy soul, doth not he know it? and shall not he render to every man according to his works?" (Proverbs 24:11, 12).

Kidner's comment on Proverbs 24:10-12 is worth noting in this connection: "Exceptional strain (10) and avoidable responsibility (11, 12) are fair tests, not unfair, of a man's mettle. It is the hireling, not the true shepherd who will plead bad conditions (10), hopeless tasks (11) and pardonable ignorance (12); love is not so lightly quieted — nor is the God of love." (Derek Kidner, *The Proverbs, An Introduction and Commentary*, [Chicago: Inter-Varsity Press, 1964], page 154.)

Delitzsch's comment on Proverbs 28:17 is very fitting here also: "Grace cannot come into the place of justice till justice has been fully recognized. Human sympathy, human forbearance, under the false title of grace, do not stand in contrast to this justice." (Franz Delitzsch, *Biblical Commentary on the Proverbs of Solomon* [Grand Rapids: Eerdmans], II, 234.) [*Institutes of Biblical Law*, pages 463-65.]

Rushdoony also deals with the principle of restitution. He points out, for example, that the thief had to make restitution to the person he harmed. In our present society, commencing with the wicked governments of the Middle Ages, the thief may be imprisoned or required to make restitution to the state; but the party who is harmed is left without recourse and is supposed to be satisfied with the idea that the thief "has been punished," as we constantly are told. Some vague thing called society seems to be the holder of the debt; and, when he has paid his debt to society, the thief is turned loose. The person deprived of his property, the virtue of a loved one, or whatever, has received no recompense whatever. And the justice and rights of God have been ignored.

In the civil code of Moses, as Rushdoony also indicates, there were three basic categories of punishment: execution, banishment and restitution. There was no provision for prisons. Sometimes—as in the case of wife-beating—a person could be publicly whipped. But prison seems to be "cruel and unusual punishment" in the eyes of God. A person was detained only for a short time while awaiting trial. Following is a small portion of Rushdoony's comments on retribution or restitution:

> The golden rule is often cited, and properly so, as a summation of the law: "Therefore all things whatsoever ye would that men should do to you, do ye even so to them: for this is the law and the prophets" (Matt. 7:12). To observe the law in relationship to our neighbor, recognizing his right to life, home, property, and reputation, is to love him, and to do to him as we would have others do unto us. Not only is this a fundamental principle of Scripture, but its reverse is equally fundamental. As Obadiah stated it, "as thou has done, it shall be done unto thee: thy reward shall return upon thine own head" (Obad. 15; cf. Judges 1:17; Ps. 137:8; Ezek. 35:15; Joel 3:7, 8).

What have corrupt judges done, and what is their

penalty? Josephus reported on the penalty: "If any judge takes bribes, his punishment is death: he that overlooks one that offers him a petition, and this when he is able to relieve him, he is a guilty person." (Flavius Josephus, *Against Apion*, II, 27; in William Whiston, *The Works of Flavius Josephus* [Philadelphia: David McKay], page 919.) Why this penalty?

An important point with respect to this law is that it is *civil* law. The impersonality required of the civil courts is markedly different from the personalism of decisions in other realms. In the family, judgments can be more lenient and more severe, depending upon the situation. The family must live with the offending member; it may be more severe if it feels he is hopeless, or more lenient if it feels the offender has learned his lesson. In the church, because believers are members of one another, the same is true. They are not to resort to the impersonality of the civil courts unless the member refuses to accept the church's discipline. In that case, he is a heathen and a publican and is dealt with impersonally (Matt. 18:7). Family and church justice is personal, and, in a sense, partial, respecting persons, although still just. In the state, where persons of varying backgrounds confront one another, impersonality and impartiality must be the rule of justice. Family and ecclesiastical justice, being personal, can be concerned with rehabilitation; civil justice must be tied to restitution only, the principle of justice. Where the state assumes a parental role, or a pastoral role, it not only usurps the jurisdictions of family and church, but also forsakes the impersonal justice it must administer. The state then becomes a class agency, or an instrument of a race or some dominant group. If it substitutes rehabilitation or punishment for restitution, it penalizes the injured party in favor of the criminal.

Within the family, an impersonal justice is fatal. For husband and wife to deal with one another impersonally is to destroy their relationship, which must be one of justice surely, but also of mutual forbearance. Every area of personal relationships is similar. But traffic laws cannot be personal, and marital laws cannot be impersonal. When ecclesiastical discipline becomes impersonal, it means, practically, excommunication. The counsel to Christians to avoid the courts against one another (1 Cor. 6:1-10) in part presupposes this requirement of justice tempered with forbearance in personal relationships. (*Institutes of Biblical Law,* pages 536-37.)

The serious student of the Old Testament will want to build a library of the most useful, authoritative and scholarly commentaries. Many old ones—such as Clarke's—have been republished in recent years and can be purchased at a reasonable price.

BOOK OF MORMON MOST VALUABLE COMMENTARY

The Old Testament as we have it is generally believed to have been put together in the sixth and fifth centuries B.C. While we know that isn't entirely true, we do know that devout Jews from that general period would be vastly more conversant with the Old Testament prophetic mind than anyone else—which is precisely what we have in such prophets as Lehi, Nephi and Jacob. And their knowledge was passed on down to their successors. They had the brass plates of Laban, which probably provided a better record of the Old Testament period up to Jeremiah's era than the Old Testament we have. So the Book of Mormon is a rich source of information about the Old Testament.

For example, the Book of Mormon establishes the fact that all the prophets worshipped Christ (as has been noted earlier in this chapter). Knowing that all the Old Testament writers were Christians and that they knew Jehovah was to be the Savior (see 3 Nephi 15:5; Isaiah 43:11; 45:15, 21; 49:26; 60:16; Hosea 13:4) has a profound effect on one's understanding of their books. The Book of Mormon settles this once and for all. Note, for example, the following Book of Mormon passages:

> Yea, and they did keep the law of Moses; for it was expedient that they should keep the law of Moses as yet, for it was not all fulfilled. But notwithstanding the law of Moses, they did look forward to the coming of Christ, considering that the law of Moses was a type of his coming, and believing that they must keep those outward performances until the time that he should be revealed unto them.
>
> Now they did not suppose that salvation came by the law of Moses; but the law of Moses did serve to strengthen their faith in Christ; and thus they did retain a hope through faith, unto eternal salvation, relying upon the spirit of prophecy, which spake of those things to come. (Alma 25: 15-16.)

> Therefore, it is expedient that there should be a great and last sacrifice; and then shall there be, or it is expedient there should be, a stop to the shedding of blood; then shall the law of Moses be fulfilled; yea, it shall be all fulfilled, every jot and tittle, and none shall have passed away.
>
> And behold, this is the whole meaning of the law, every whit pointing to that great and last sacrifice; and that great and last sacrifice will be the Son of God, yea, infinite and eternal.
>
> And thus he shall bring salvation to all those who shall believe on his name; this being the intent of this last sacrifice, to bring about the bowels of mercy, which overpowereth justice, and bringeth about means unto men that they may have faith unto repentance. (Alma 34:13-15.)

This Christian flavor of the Old Testament is established by the Book of Mormon, not only as it applies to the period of the law of Moses but also from Moses on back to Abraham and earlier. (See, for example, Helaman 8:11-20.)

The Book of Mormon establishes the historical reality of many events mentioned in the Old Testament. For example, the second chapter of 2 Nephi, along with many other passages throughout the Book of Mormon, establishes the fact of the fall of Adam. Verse 22 is especially important because it eliminates any question about the universal effect of the Fall. Father Lehi says specifically that "all things which were created must have remained in the same state in which they were after they were created; and they would have remained forever, and had no end." It would be hard to come up with language which would more pointedly state the universality of the Fall—that is, that all life went from an immortal state to a mortal state. Further, Lehi's use of the phrases "and they would have remained forever, and had no end" eliminates any question about the state of the world and all in it before the Fall: All was immortal.

The way we got the Book of Mormon eliminates any possibility of treating this account as the world in general treats the biblical account of the Fall—that it is a record of legends handed down from primitive men. If the Book of Mormon had been discovered by a world famous archaeologist and translated by a group of the world's best linguists, it could be treated much the same way the Bible is treated. For some, it might increase faith in the Bible just as the Dead Sea Scrolls have increased the faith of some; but it would not essentially change the basic attitudes of the world. Nor could it be used as a basis of setting up The Church of Jesus Christ of Latter-day Saints. The Book of Mormon did not come that way. It came by the power of God through the instrumentality of angels, miracles, and divine instruments. It was designed and nursed through the ages by God. And, when it had been translated, the voice of the Lord was heard by witnesses saying, "The book is true and the translation is correct."

Another Bible story which has been generally doubted and relegated to myth is the story of the confusion of tongues at the Tower of Babel. The story of the Jaredites exonerates the Genesis account. (See Ether 1:3, 33; Omni 22.) Also, many, if not most, look upon the account of the miracles of the exodus from Egypt as embellishment of facts that might have a more natural explanation if we knew what really happened. In 1 Nephi 4:2 and 17:27, we learn that the waters of the Red Sea were parted "hither and thither." When Nephi was being persecuted by his brethren in the wilderness, he gave a long account of many of the miracles that God had performed for Moses and the Israelites. (See 1 Nephi 17:24-42.) This same account includes verification of some of the miracles that were performed in the wilderness during the forty years of wandering, and it also establishes the fact that it was God who commanded the Israelites to displace the Canaanites. It also gives the reasons for this unusual treatment of the Canaanites.

One of the most unusual accounts in the Bible, and one that has strained the credulity of millions of supposedly enlightened people, is that of Joshua commanding the sun not to go down. (Joshua 10:12-14.) This, too, is verified by the Book of Mormon. (See Helaman 12:14, 15.) And one cannot argue that this was just a superstition the Nephites brought with them from the Old World. One must always remember that the Lord often prevented things from being included in the record and insisted on other things being added. And he approved of the final product.

Furthermore, the very context of the Helaman account (it was apparently an editorial comment by Mormon) eliminates any possibility that the writer could have fallen into any such error. The writer is recounting miracles and physical phenomena deliberately to illustrate the power of God. He is describing the kind of cosmology a true Saint must believe in — a cosmology in which God intervenes and actively participates in events to bring about his purposes. Cataclysms occur. The earth is flooded completely to accomplish a baptism of water. It will undergo a baptism of fire. Continents are wrenched apart and will be brought back together. Mountains are thrown up in a matter of minutes, and the sea is heaved beyond its bounds. Whole nations are destroyed in an instant; and another nation, Israel, while punished suitably, is preserved miraculously many times. Mormon is not recounting superstitions. He is seriously describing the reasons we must not take the power of God lightly. And this is the same Mormon who was told to put the "Small Plates" in the record for "a wise purpose" (Words of Mormon 1:7) and who was told not to include other things. (See, for example, 3 Nephi 26:11.)

Elsewhere in this book reference has been made to other ways in which the Book of Mormon supports the Bible. For instance, chapter one shows how the Book of Mormon establishes Isaiah as the sole author of the book bearing his name. The careful student of the Book of Mormon and the Bible (one must read both to see how they support each other) will discover a multitude of passages in the former that shed light on the interpretation of the latter. Following is a list of the kinds of things that can be found:

1. Why were the Canaanites deprived of the Promised Land? (See 1 Nephi 17:32-35.)

2. What was the meaning of the brazen serpent on a

staff raised up by Moses in the wilderness? (See 1 Nephi 17:41; 2 Nephi 25:20; Alma 33:19-22; Helaman 8:14, 15.)

3. How did Jacob (son of Isaac) know that some of Joseph's posterity would die and some would be saved? (See Alma 46:23-26.)

4. What light does the Book of Mormon shed on the meaning of the sealed book prophecy as contained in Isaiah 29? (See 2 Nephi 26 and 27.)

5. How do we know that plural marriage is wicked unless commanded by God to raise up seed to him? (See Jacob 2:30.)

6. To whose feet did Isaiah have reference when he said, "How beautiful upon the mountain are the feet of him that bringeth good tidings?" (See Mosiah 15:11-19.)

MODERN REVELATIONS GIVE COMMENTARY ON OLD TESTAMENT

The Book of Mormon is a record written by peculiarly Jewish prophets who, unlike the Nephites generally, were well conversant with the manner of prophesying among the Jews (2 Nephi 25:1, 4). The Latter-day Saints are blessed with inspired commentary even on top of that. We have the Inspired Version of the Bible, which contains many corrections and restorations to the original text. The Inspired Version has not been canonized by the Church; that is, the Saints are not under a covenant through common consent to accept it on the same level of authority as the Book of Mormon, the Doctrine and Covenants and the Pearl of Great Price. But some parts of it are in the Pearl of Great Price, and these parts have been accepted by covenant as a standard of truth. The Book of Moses came to us in this way. Also, we have the Book of Abraham, translated by Joseph Smith from a papyrus roll, which sheds a great deal of light on the Old Testament. We learn from it, as well as from Moses 1, that the ancients were far more learned in mathematics and astronomy than was once believed. From the second facsimile (pages 34-35) we learn that Abraham possessed a knowledge of time-distance relationships which the world in general believes did not come to light until Einstein's work on relativity. (See also Joseph Smith's statement about the relativity of time in D&C 88:42-44.)

The Doctrine and Covenants contains many phrases that are similar or identical to statements in the Bible, especially from the writings of Moses, Isaiah and other prophets. Section 113 is a commentary on Isaiah 11. Section 77 deals with the time span from the Fall to the final judgment. Section 133 has thirty-eight footnotes to Old Testament passages. Many other sections are footnoted to the Old Testament. Verses 47-54 in section 45 explain and add light to Zechariah 13:6 as well as to other parts of Zechariah. And the list could go on and on.

The Latter-day Saint Old Testament student must not lose sight of the value he can get from the light which modern revelation sheds on the New Testament, and how this, in turn, sheds light on the Old Testament. For example, Jacob chapters 5 and 6 explain the allegory of the tame and wild olive trees. This increases understanding about the Old Testament directly in that it explains the Lord's plans for the house of Israel throughout history. It also adds clarity to such New Testament passages as Romans 11:11-24 and many verses in chapters one and two of Ephesians. It is the foundation for the doctrine of election and the secret plans of God to control the destinies of all nations without interfering with the free agency of individuals within them. This doctrine also brings a unity to the Old and New Testaments that is otherwise absent. The more one understands the fifth chapter of Jacob, the more he can see that the New Testament episode was just a continuation of the Lord's workings with the house of Israel to bring salvation to all people. And he can see how the work with the Gentiles of that day was one of the graftings-in of the wild branches onto the tame tree.

Perhaps the best way to conclude this chapter and this book is to reemphasize and reiterate the need for all Saints to read and study the Old Testament. One could study the Old Testament for a lifetime and never plumb its depths. But that is no excuse to turn away from it; in fact, quite the opposite. It is reason to give the Old Testament careful and constant attention.

One more idea cannot be stressed enough: Old Testament scholars who are not steeped in a knowledge of the Book of Mormon cannot begin to know and understand the Old Testament to the degree that they will if they study the Book of Mormon constantly. In a slightly different but equally important way, the same can be said of all modern revelation. No Old Testament scholar will be fully vindicated in his comments and conclusions. Each will err in some particular or another. But each new truth unearthed will vindicate and corroborate the Book of Mormon and the modern prophets as they have shed light on the Old Testament and the ancient people who walk through its pages.

SELECTED BIBLIOGRAPHY

Alexander, David, and Alexander, Pat, eds. *Eerdmans Handbook to the Bible.* Grand Rapids, Mi.: Wm. B. Eerdmans Publishing Company, 1973.

Atlas of the Bible Lands. Maplewood, N.J.: C. S. Hammond and Company, 1969.

Berrett, LaMar C. *Discovering the World of the Bible.* Provo, Ut.: The Young House, 1973.

Budge, Wallis. *Egyptian Religion.* 2d ed. New York: Bell Publishing Company, 1959.

Clarke, Adam. *The Holy Bible Containing the Old and New Testaments.* 6 vols. Nashville: Abingdon Press, n.d.

Douglas, J. D., ed. *The New Bible Dictionary.* Grand Rapids, Mi.: Wm. B. Eerdmans Publishing Company, 1962.

Dummelow, J. R., ed. *A Commentary on the Holy Bible.* New York: Macmillan Company, 1936.

Edersheim, Alfred. *Bible History: Old Testament.* Grand Rapids, Mi.: Wm. B. Eerdmans Publishing Company, 1972.

————. *The Temple: Its Ministry and Services.* Grand Rapids, Mi.: Wm. B. Eerdmans Publishing Company, 1976.

Encyclopedia Judaica. 16 vols. Keter Publishing House Jerusalem Ltd., 1972.

Guthrie, D., and Motyer, J. A., eds. *The New Bible Commentary.* Rev. ed. Grand Rapids, Mi.: Wm. B. Eerdmans Publishing Company, 1970.

Josephus, Flavius. *The Life and Works of Flavius Josephus.* Translated by William Whiston. New York: Holt, Rinehart, and Winston, n.d.

Journal of Discourses. 26 vols. London: Latter-day Saints' Book Depot, 1854-86.

Keil, C. F., and Delitzsch, F. *Commentary on the Old Testament.* 25 vols. Grand Rapids, Mi.: Wm. B. Eerdmans Publishing Company, 1978.

McConkie, Bruce R. *Doctrinal New Testament Commentary.* 3 vols. Salt Lake City: Bookcraft, 1965-73.

————. *The Promised Messiah: The First Coming of Christ.* Salt Lake City: Deseret Book Company, 1978.

————. "When Thou Art Converted, Strengthen Thy Brethren." *Study Guide for Melchizedek Priesthood Quorums of the Church 1974-75.* Salt Lake City: The Church of Jesus Christ of Latter-day Saints, 1974.

McKay, David O. "The Atonement," *The Instructor* (March 1959): 65-66.

Matthews, Robert J. *A Plainer Translation: Joseph Smith's Translation of the Bible.* Provo, Ut.: Brigham Young University Press, 1975.

Nibley, Hugh. *Lehi in the Desert and The World of the Jaredites.* Salt Lake City: Bookcraft, 1952.

————. *Messages of the Joseph Smith Papyri: An Egyptian Endowment.* Salt Lake City: Deseret Book Company, 1975.

Petersen, Mark E. *Adam: Who Is He?* Salt Lake City: Deseret Book Company, 1976.

Rasmussen, Ellis T. *Patriarchs of the Old Testament.* Sunday School Gospel Doctrine Course Manual. Salt Lake City: Deseret Sunday School Union, 1964.

Rushdoony, Rousas John. *Institutes of Biblical Law.* Presbyterian and Reformed Publishing Company, 1973.

Skousen, W. Cleon. *The First 2000 Years*. Salt Lake City: Bookcraft, 1953.

———. *The Fourth Thousand Years*. Salt Lake City: Bookcraft, 1966.

———. *The Third Thousand Years*. Salt Lake City: Bookcraft, 1964.

Smith, Joseph, Jr. *History of The Church of Jesus Christ of Latter-day Saints*. Edited by B. H. Roberts. 7 vols. Salt Lake City: The Church of Jesus Christ of Latter-day Saints, 1949.

———. *Teachings of the Prophet Joseph Smith*. Compiled by Joseph Fielding Smith. Salt Lake City: Deseret Book Company, 1938.

Smith, Joseph Fielding. *Doctrines of Salvation*. Compiled by Bruce R. McConkie. 3 vols. Salt Lake City: Bookcraft, 1954-56.

Sperry, Sidney B. *The Spirit of the Old Testament*. 2d ed. revised and enlarged. Salt Lake City: Deseret Book Company, 1970.

———. *The Voice of Israel's Prophets*. Salt Lake City: Deseret Book Company, 1952.

INDEX

Poetry, 48-49, 187
Polytheism, 11
Postexilic day, 2
Premortal life, 84
Priests, ancient, 29, 152, 159
"Priest's Manual," 29
Prisons, 213
Promised land, 86, 91
Prophecies, 168-70;
    double meaning of, 185;
    nature of, 185-86;
    spirit of, 200
Prophets, clothing of, 182-83;
    the Lord's relationship with, 17;
    major, 56-62;
    minor, 62-72
Proverbs, 49, 52-53
Psalms, 49, 51-52, 188
Ptolemies, 133
Punishment, 213
Purpose of life, 143
Pyramids, 109-10

— R —

Rams, in offerings, 150, 159;
    symbol of, 185
Reading, 166-67
Record keeping, 43
Refining, figurative meaning of, 181
Rehoboam, 95
Restitution, 212-13
Ruth, 37-38

— S —

Sacrifice, 65, 138;
    animal, 144-45;
    figurative meaning of, 182;
    ordinance of, 141-43
Salem, city of, 84
Salt, 146, 154
Samaria, 98
Samaritans, 45

Samuel, First and Second, 37, 38-40,
    90-91
Samuel, writings of, 34
Satan, 197
Saul, 39-40, 91
"Scapegoat," 160
Scattering of Israel, 134
Scholars, 1
Scholarship, 16
Scribes, 44, 106
Scripture study, 164-65
Scythians, 131
Sea People, 125, 127
Segregation, 207-8
Selfishness, 143
Self-mutilation, 146
Septuagint, 3, 7, 26
Serpent of brass, 171
Seven (number), 160
Sheep, in offerings, 151
Shekhinah, 181-82
Sin offering, 147-49
"Slaughter," figurative expression of,
    182
Smith, Joseph, linguistic ability, 16
Solomon, 42, 52-53, 93-94, 119, 123
Song of Solomon, 21, 54-55
Southern Kingdom. *See* Judah
Spirit world, 196
Spiritual, all things, 53
Spirituality, 77
Suffering, 59-60
"Sweet savor" offering, 144
Synagogues, 103
Syria, 97

— T —

Tabernacle, 28-29
Tattooing, 202
Taxation, 195
Temples, 70, 159, 181
Ten Commandments, 28, 32
Ten tribes. *See* Tribes of Israel

Ten tribes (kingdom). *See* Northern
 Kingdom
Theocratic governments, 90
Theodicy, 50
Threshing, 178
Time cues, 167-70
Torah, 21
Tower of Babel, 218
Transjordan kingdoms, 120-35
Translated beings, 84
Trespass offering, 149-50
Tribes of Israel, 89, 99, 119, 130, 168

— U —

United States Constitution, 2
Ur, 129

— V —

Veil, 160

Vintage, figurative meaning of, 179
Vocabulary, 167
"Voluntary" offerings, 144

— W —

"Water," figurative meaning of, 177
"Wind," figurative meaning of, 177
Winepress, 179
"Wisdom literature," 21, 49

— Z —

Zechariah, 55, 70-71
Zenock, 8
Zenos, 7-8
Zephaniah, 55, 69
Zionic city. *See* City of Enoch